Edmund Burke, William Burke

An account of the European settlements in America in six parts.

Each part contains an accurate description of the settlements in it, their extent,

climate, productions, trade genius and disposition of their inhabitants: the interests

of the several - Vol. 2

Edmund Burke, William Burke

An account of the European settlements in America in six parts.
Each part contains an accurate description of the settlements in it, their extent, climate, productions, trade genius and disposition of their inhabitants: the interests of the several - Vol. 2

ISBN/EAN: 9783337775216

Printed in Europe, USA, Canada, Australia, Japan

Cover: Foto ©ninafisch / pixelio.de

More available books at **www.hansebooks.com**

AN ACCOUNT

OF THE

Europеan Settlements

IN

AMERICA.

IN SIX PARTS.

I. A fhort Hiftory of the Difcovery of that Part of the World.
II. The Manners and Cuftoms of the original Inhabitants.
III. Of the Spanifh Settlements.
IV. Of the Portuguefe.
V. Of the French, Dutch, and Danifh.
VI. Of the Englifh.

Each PART contains

An accurate Defcription of the Settlements in it, their Extent, Climate, Productions, Trade, Genius and Difpofition of their Inhabitants: the Interefts of the feveral Powers of Europe with refpect to thofe Settlements; and their Political and Commercial Views with regard to each other.

VOL. II.

The THIRD EDITION, with IMPROVEMENTS.

LONDON:
Printed for R. and J. DODSLEY in Pall-Mall.

MDCCLX.

THE CONTENTS

Of the Second Volume.

PART V.

The French Settlements.

CHAP. I.

THE time in which the French began their West-India settlements. Favoured by cardinal Richlieu. De Poincy governor. The West-India company. page 3

CHAP. II.

The destruction of the colony of St. Christopher's. The rise of the buccaneers. The cause of their success. The settlement of Hispaniola. The policy of France. A description of Hispaniola. Its trade. The towns of Cape Francoise and Leogan. 9

CHAP. III.

A description of Martinico. Of Guardaloupe and other French islands. Their produce. Observations on the mistakes that have been made about their value. 19

CHAP. IV.

French North America. Description of Canada. Its climate. The fair of Montreal.

CONTENTS.

Real. Quebec. The inhabitants of Canada. The river St. Laurence and the great lakes. Cape Breton. 25

CHAP. V.

Louisiana. The Missisippi. The Ohio. The fountain of youth. The colony of Louisiana. 35

CHAP. VI.

The French policy with regard to their colonies. 40

CHAP. VII.

The Dutch settlements. Curassou. The city, its trade. The Spanish counterband. Eustatia. The Danish company. The Danish island of Santa Cruz. The characters of the several European nations as they regard America. 50

PART VI.

The English Settlements.

CHAP. I.

The division of the English West-Indies. Description of Jamaica. Conquest of that island. 59

CHAP.

CONTENTS.

CHAP. II.

The settlement of Jamaica. The failure of cacao. The buccaneers. The flourishing state of that island. Its decline in some respects.
67

CHAP. III.

The products of Jamaica. Piemento. Sugar. Rum. Molasses. Cotton. Ginger. The logwood trade. Disputes about it. The counterband. Slave trade.
70

CHAP. IV.

Port-Royal. The earthquake 1692. Kingston. St. Jago de la Vega, or Spanish-town. Disputes about the removal of the seat of government.
79

CHAP. V.

Barbadoes. Its savage condition at the first planting. The hardships suffered by the planters. The speedy increase of the island. Its great wealth and number of inhabitants. Its decline. Present state of the island.
84

A 3 CHAP.

CONTENTS.

CHAP. VI.

St. Chriſtopher, Antegua, Nevis, Montſerrat; their preſent condition and force. 91

CHAP. VII.

Climate of the Weſt-Indies. The rains and winds. Hurricanes. Their prognoſtics. Produce of the Weſt-Indies. Sugar. The manner of manufacturing it. Planters in the Weſt-Indies. Their way of life and management of their affairs. The Negroes. 94

CHAP. VIII.

Obſervations on the ſettlement of the Weſt-Indies. Advantages there for tempers prejudicial at home. Bad tempers not always noxious in every ſenſe. 106

CHAP. IX.

Obſervations on taxing the colonies. On an expenſive eſtabliſhment there. Objections anſwered. 110

CHAP. X.

State of the negroes in the Weſt-Indies. Danger from them. Methods propoſed for remedying

CONTENTS.

ing these abuses. The necessity of increasing the whites. Use of this rgulation in trade. 116

CHAP. XI.

Misery of the negroes. Great waste of them. Methods of preventing it. Instruction of negroes in religion. 124

CHAP. XII.

Proposal for a sort of enfranchisement of mulattoes and negroes. Danger from the multitude of house negroes. 130

PART VII.

British North America.

CHAP. I.

A general view of the English dominions in North America. 134

CHAP. II.

First attempts to settle North America. The rise and progress of the puritans. They are persecuted by Laud. Several fly into New England. 138

CHAP.

CONTENTS.

CHAP. III.

Difference in religion, divides the colony. Maſ-ſachuſet. Connecticut. Providence. Spirit of perſecution. Perſecution of the quakers. Diſputes about grace. 146

CHAP. IV.

The Witchcraft deluſion. Great cruelties. The madneſs ends in the accuſation of the magiſtrates. Reflections. 155

CHAP. V.

The ſituation, climate, &c. of New England. Indian corn deſcribed. Cattle of New England. 162

CHAP. VI.

People of New England. Their numbers. Hiſtory of the charters of the colonies here, and the forfeiture of ſome. 167

CHAP. VII.

Boſton, its harbour. Trade. Ship-building. Diſtillery. Foreign traffic. Reflections on the ſcheme of limiting it. Declenſion of the trade of New England. 171

CHAP.

CONTENTS.

CHAP. VIII.

New York, New Jersey, and Pensylvania. Description of their situation, &c. Short account of their settlement. 184

CHAP. IX.

City of New York. Its flourishing trade. Albany. The Indian trade there. The Iroquois or Six Nations. 190

CHAP. X.

New Jersey. Its trade; and inhabitants. 194

CHAP. XI.

Account of William Pen. The principles on which he settled the colony. His death. 195

CHAP. XII.

Inhabitants of Pensylvania. Variety of nations and religions there. Pacific principles of the quakers. Reflections on the present state of affairs there. 199

CHAP. XIII.

Description of Philadelphia. Its trade. Number of people in Pensylvania. Its flourishing condition. Few negroes there. 203

CONTENTS.

CHAP. XIV.

Situation, &c. of Virginia. Conveniency of its rivers for navigation. Beasts and birds of the country. The opossum. 206

CHAP. XV.

Towns in Virginia few and small. Tobacco, its cultivation. Trade in that and other commodities. People in Virginia. White and black. 212

CHAP. XVI.

Attempts to settle Virginia, three unsuccessful. Settled at last by lord Delawar. 217

CHAP. XVII.

Virginia holds out against Cromwell, and is reduced. Bacon's rebellion. Its causes. Bacon dies. Peace restored. 222

CHAP. XVIII.

Maryland. The time of settling it. Grant to lord Baltimore. Attempts of king James to deprive him of his jurisdiction. He is deprived of it on the revolution. He is restored. Capital of Maryland. Its trade and inhabitants. 226

CHAP.

CONTENTS.

CHAP. XIX.

Attempts of the French to settle Carolina. They are beat off by the Spaniards. 233

CHAP. XX.

Carolina is settled by the English. Its constitution. The lords proprietors resign their charter. Made a royal government, and divided into two provinces. 236

CHAP. XXI.

Situation, climate, &c. of Carolina. Its animal and vegetable productions. 241

CHAP. XXII.

The commodities of Carolina for export. Rice, indigo, pitch and tar. Process in raising and manufacturing these commodities. 246

CHAP. XXIII.

North Carolina, some account of its settlement. Bad state of that province. Is considerably improved. Chief town. 255

CHAP. XXIV.

An account of Charles-town. Port-Royal. The trade of Carolina. Its vast increase. Articles not sufficiently attended to there. 257

CHAP.

CONTENTS.

CHAP. XXV.

Settlement of Georgia. Reasons for it. The plan of the settlement defective. Attempts to remedy it. 263

CHAP. XXVI.

Colony new modelled. Faults in the new constitution. Trade of this province. 269

CHAP. XXVII.

Nova Scotia, the time and reasons of its settlement. French there. Climate and soil. Annapolis, Halifax and Lunenburg. 273

CHAP. XXVIII.

The island of Newfoundland. The fishery there. The Bermudas. Their settlement and trade. The Bahamas. 280

CHAP. XXIX.

Hudson's Bay. Attempts for the discovery of a North-West passage. The Hudson's bay company. Thoughts upon its trade. Climate and soil of the countries there. Conclusion. 285

CHAP. XXX.

The royal, proprietary, and charter governments. Laws of the colonies. Paper currency. Abuses in it. Another sort of money proposed. 296

AN

AN ACCOUNT

OF THE

EUROPEAN SETTLEMENTS

IN

AMERICA.

VOL. II.

B

ACCOUNT

AMERICA

PART V.

The French Settlements.

CHAP. I.

The time in which the French began their West-India settlements. Favoured by cardinal Richlieu. De Poincy governor. The West-India company.

THE French were amongst the last nations who made settlements in the West-Indies; but they made ample amends by the vigour with which they pursued them, and by that chain of judicious and admirable measures which they used in drawing from them every advantage, which the nature of the climate would yield; and in contending against the difficulties which it threw in their way.

The civil wars, which divided and harrassed that kingdom, from the death of Henry the second, with very little interruption, until the majority of Lewis the fourteenth, withdrew the attention of both prince and people from their commercial interests to those of parties in religion and government. The politics of the house of Valois, though France perhaps was never governed by princes of so ingenious and refined a turn, were wholly of the Machiavillian kind. They tended to distract, to unsettle, to try dangerous schemes, and to raise storms only to display a skill in pilotage. The parties then in France solely contended, what power could be given to or taken from the king, without considering what could make their country a great kingdom. Therefore, which way soever the balance inclined, whether to the king or to the nobles, to the catholics or to the protestants, it was pretty indifferent to the real happiness of that nation. The parties only gamed out of a common stock. Neither could be enriched. But their dissensions made all of them poor and weak. The time of cardinal Richlieu must be considered as the true æra of French policy. This great man pacifying all at home, exalting the royal authority upon the ruins of the power of the nobility, and modelling that great system of general policy in external affairs, which has raised France to such a pitch

pitch of greatness; amongst so many, and such extensive cares, did not forget those of commerce, and what serves most effectually to support commerce, colonies, and establishments abroad. But the circumstances of the time, and his genius that embraced so many objects, did not leave him leisure to perfect what he began. It was reserved for that great, wise, and honest minister Colbert, one of the ablest that ever served any prince, or honoured any country, to bring that plan to perfection, to carry it in a great measure into execution, and to leave things in such order, that it was not difficult, when favourable circumstances offered, to make France one of the first trading powers in Europe, and her colonies the most powerful, their nature considered, of any in America.

So early as the reign of Francis I. the French attempted an establishment in North-America; but it was not until the year 1625, that they made their first settlement in the West-Indies. This was upon St. Christopher, one of the Caribbee islands. A remarkable circumstance attended it; the English took possession of the island the same day. But this settlement had not long life on either side. The Spaniards had reason to dread the establishment of such powers in their neighbourhood; and they envied the French and English those advantages it was foreseen they would draw from countries from which they had themselves no benefit, and which they claimed only to keep them deserts.

They assaulted these new colonies, and drove them out of the island. The English colony soon returned, and possessed themselves of the largest and most fertile quarter, before the French could collect themselves; who, finding the English already occupied the best part, left a small colony on the other. But their chief, and the most adventurous of their inhabitants, went in search of a new settlement; when, after various fortune, and after combating the difficulties which an uncultivated country and some indiscretions of their own had caused them, they made a considerable settlement in the islands of Martinico and Guardaloupe.

Cardinal Richlieu saw very early into the advantages which might arise from these settlements, if prudently managed; and he thought the most prudent management both for securing and extending them, consisted in but one article; which was, to put the government into proper hands. With that view he made choice of Monsieur de Poincy, a knight of Malta; who was sent thither with the title of governor and lieutenant-general of the isles of America, and a very ample commission. No person could be better fitted to rectify the disorders that naturally must arise in every new settlement, and to put things in a right channel for the time to come. Of a good family;

family; of an unblemished reputation for probity; of great reading; of much and various knowledge of life; and of a genius as variously exercised. He was a master in mechanical learning; in which he excelled not more to his own honour, than to the benefit of the colonies which had the happiness to be committed to his care. He it was that first taught them the method of cultivating the sugar cane, and preparing the sugar. He improved the methods which were used in the Brazils for this purpose, both with regard to the mills and the furnaces; and having given a direction to their industry, he gave it all the encouragement he could, by supporting those who raised their own substance, by the means which advanced the colony; whilst he kept a watchful eye, and a severe hand upon all, who were for making hasty fortunes, without adding to the public stock. He made admirable regulations for the speedy and impartial administration of justice; and knowing that all order must depend for its blessing above, and its effect here upon an attention to religion, he ordered a proper number of churches to be built in all the islands under his care, and settled priests in them, with a competent, but not a superfluous provision; but he did not think monasteries and monks so compatible with a new colony.

Under the infpection of this governor, Martinico, Guardaloupe, part of St. Chriftopher's, St. Bartholomew, and St. Martin, were fettled, and began to flourifh, and that with very little help from home. A plain proof that almoft every thing depends in affairs of this nature, on chufing proper men to command, and giving them a proper authority.

Thefe iflands, however, were unhappily under the fuperintendance of an exclufive company, which, in fpite of all that could otherwife be done, efpecially after the death of Richlieu, fo neglected, or mifmanaged their affairs, that they were obliged to fell a part of the fettlements; and they left the reft hardly worth purchafing. But the government at length bought up the iflands which they had alienated, and refcued the others out of their hands. The trade under proper regulations was laid open, yet protected under the wings of their great India company. Thefe regulations took place about 1680, and the benefits of this arrangement were great, and foon apparent. Exclufive companies may probably be ufeful to nourifh an infant trade. They may be ufeful too for a very diftant one, where the market is to be nicely managed, and where it is under the dominion of foreign and barbarous princes. But where the trade is between different parts of the dominions of

the

the same prince, under the protection of his laws, carried on by his own subjects, and with goods wrought in his own country, such companies must be equally absurd in their nature, and ruinous in their consequences to the trade.

CHAP. II.

The destruction of the colony of St. Christopher's. The rise of the buccaneers. The cause of their success. The settlement of Hispaniola. The policy of France. A description of Hispaniola. Its trade. The towns of Cape Francoise and Leogan.

AFTER the Spaniards had ruined the first colony at St. Christopher's, they brought upon themselves by this act, a very heavy revenge for the injustice of it. Their example at the same time made it apparent, how much better it is to let a bold and adventurous people settle in some place where they can do but little mischief, and to suffer their spirit to evaporate in peaceful occupations, rather than to keep it up by difficulties, unable to quell it, but which may force it to take another and more dangerous turn.

Several of the French inhabitants, who were expelled from St. Christopher's, being reduced to great indigence, began to think of desperate courses.

courses. They betook themselves to piracy; and uniting with some vagrant English, Dutch, and other outcasts of all nations, but resolute fellows, and not destitute of men of capacity amongst them, they began a piratical war upon the Spaniards. At first they satisfied themselves with taking their ships and destroying their trade; which they did effectually; but soon encouraged and strengthened by this success, they landed upon the continent of New-Spain and Terra Firma, burning and plundering the open country. Their boldness and number increasing with their success, they assaulted and took some of their strongest fortresses and most opulent towns. They took Portobello, Campeachy, Maracaibo, Gibraltar, and the fortress of Chagra; they even took the city of Panama by storm, and burned it, after defeating an army which came to beat them off. In all which places, and in the others which they had taken, they gained an incredible booty, and committed the most unheard-of cruelties. Another party of these pirates passed the streights of Magellan, and entering into the South-Sea, turned the whole coast of Peru, Chili, and the East of Mexico, into one scene of desolation; every where attended with success, because every where acting with a bravery and conduct, that in any other cause had merited the highest honours.

It

It is not a little surprising, at first view, that all the great things which were done in this new world, were either done by actual pirates, as these men were, or by private adventures, but one degree better authorized, and nothing better supported; whose own courage and skill were to be at once their commission, their magazines, and their treasury; being obliged to find the resources of the war, in the war itself. When the most numerous and the best provided armaments have shamefully failed, and failed in those very places, where the adventurers had shewn them such a glorious example of success. But the cause is not so hard to be assigned. None but men of great enterprise and bravery, conceive those expeditions of themselves. Unsupported, but at the same time unchecked by the higher powers, they were under the necessity of turning to every side, and of exerting every faculty. But then they had nothing to hinder this exertion. Their first attempts were generally low, and therefore they were prosperous. They did not lead great armies to be subsisted with great difficulty, and to be discouraged and wasted by the hardships of the climate; but they habituated themselves to hardships by degrees: they were encouraged by smaller successes; and having nothing to expect from their power and numbers, they made amends by their vigilance, their activity, and their courage.

courage. These are causes adequate to the effect; indeed adequate to any effect. Whereas in the regular way, a general of the first note and reputation has rarely been sent into America; the service seemed beneath him; and they that were tolerably expert at second and third parts, (worse than the absolutely inexperienced for the very first, where the scene is new,) were sent by court favour and intrigue. What armaments from England, Holland, and France, have been sent in different times to America, whose remains returned without honour or advantage, is too clear, and perhaps too invidious a topic to be greatly insisted upon.

The pirates, whom we called buccaneers improperly, the French denominated flibustiers, from the Dutch flyboats, in which they made their first expeditions. The buccaneers are no more than persons who hunt wild cattle in America for their hides and tallow. Some of these joined the flibustiers in their first expeditions; and from them we named the whole body, buccaneers. These people brought their prizes and plunder frequently into Jamaica, by which they enriched that island extremely. Others, finding that the Spaniards were very weak in Hispaniola, and that they had in a manner deserted a considerable part of the island, made it a place of rendezvous. They who hunted cattle saw
the

the hideous deſarts left by the Spaniſh tyranny, a proper place for exerciſing their profeſſion. To theſe two ſorts of people were ſoon added a third; who were ſome of the French in the Leſſer Antilles, who finding how much might be made by ſupplying a ſort of people who expended largely, and were not very exact in their bargains, and perceiving that no part of America afforded a better ſoil, paſſed over to this iſland, and exerciſed here their buſineſs of planters and merchants. Theſe three ſorts of people mutually in want of each other, lived in very good harmony. The Spaniards diſlodged them ſeveral times; but they ſtill returned, and with new ſtrength; ſo that it was with difficulty, and after a long diſpute, that the Spaniards were able to retain one part of the iſland.

The court of France ſaw the progreſs of theſe people ſilently. Whenever complaints were made, they diſavowed their proceedings; reſolved not to break meaſures with Spain for the ſake of an object, which they were not ſure they could hold, and the advantages of which were yet doubtful; but when they found the French in Hiſpaniola numerous, ſtrong, and wealthy, they owned them as ſubjects, ſent them a governor and regular forces to keep them ſo, and to defend them in what they had done: the old method of piracy was ſtill connived at, whilſt the trade
of

of skins increased, and the plantations extended. At last the French obtained a legal right by the cession, which the Spaniards made them of the North-West part of the island, by the treaty of Ryswick, in 1697; the best and most fertile part of the best and most fertile island in the West-Indies, and perhaps in the world; that which was the first settled, and the whole of which is upwards of four hundred miles long, and one hundred and forty broad. This is the principle settlement of the French in the West-Indies, and indeed in all America. The country is mixed; pretty mountainous in some parts, but many of these mountains are fertile, and covered with beautiful woods. Others, which are barren and rocky, anciently had mines of gold; they are not worked now, though it is judged they not only contain those of gold, but mines of silver, copper, and iron. But the French think, and I believe, with reason, that their labour is better bestowed on the culture of the plains for these rich commodities, which vend so well in Europe, than in the pursuit of mines, really more precarious in their profits, and which yield a wealth after all, of a less useful kind.

This country has likewise prodigiously fine plains, of a vast extent, and extreme fertility; either covered with noble and beautiful forests of timber and fruit-trees, excellent in their kinds, or pastured by vast numbers of horned cattle, sheep, and hogs. The air in Hispaniola is is of the most healthy in the west-Indies. The country is admirably watered with rivulets as well as navigable rivers. It is no wonder therefore, that this active and industrious nation, in possession of so excellent and extensive a country, has reaped from it prodigious advantages. They were the better enabled to do this, from the great encouragement their settlements met with in France; and from the wise regulations which were made concerning them. These we shall consider in their place. But it is certain they reckoned in the year 1726, that on this island they had no less than one hundred thousand negroes, and thirty thousand whites; that they made sixty thousand hogsheads of sugar of five hundred weight each; that the indigo was half as much in value as the sugar; that they exported large quantities of cotton, and that they had sent besides to France cacao and ginger in tolerable plenty. Since that time they have raised coffee here to a very great amount. And not this article only, but every other branch of their commercial products has increased to a degree truly astonishing since that period. Towards the conclusion of the late war a Spanish writer of great judgment and well informed, reckons the produce of the plantations near Cape St. Francoise, the capital of French Hispaniola, and which were exported from that single town, at 30,000 tons in sugar, indigo, tobacco, and coffee.

This export at the lowest possible calculation cannot be of less value than 600,000 pounds sterling. If to this we add the exports of the two considerable ports of Leogane and Petit Guaves, and the other inferior ones, which certainly do not send out less than the capital; on this low estimation, we find the exported produce of this island to be worth 1200,000l. annually; which great as it is, is certainly under-rated. But there is another branch of their trade if possible more advantageous to the mother country, the counterband which they carry on with the Spaniards, wholly in the manufactures of France, and for which they receive their returns in silver. The abovementioned author from the most authentic information tells us, that this trade returns annually to France no less than two millions of dollars. This progress of the French colonies, and their flourishing state after a war in which they suffered greatly, I have displayed, in order to explode a notion which prevails with many; that by distressing the French in time of war it is in our power entirely to destroy their commerce; but this notion, if it should prevail generally, may mislead us greatly to our disadvantage.

Nations like France and England, full of people of spirit, and of industry, easily recover all the losses of war. The trade of France was in a deplorable condition at the treaty of Utrecht. She had not then five hundred vessels of all

sorts

forts in the world. At the beginning of the last war, but thirty years after, they had eighteen hundred. Their losses in that war were very great; and yet their losses in this shew, that in a very little time they have more than repaired them. Wherever the vital principle subsists in full vigour, wounds are soon healed. Disorders themselves are a species of remedies; and every new loss not only shews how it may be repaired, but by the vigour it inspires, makes new advantages known. Such losses renew the spirit of industry and enterprise; they reduce things to their first principles; they keep alive motion; and make the appetites of traders sharp and keen. While the spitit of trade subsists, trade itself can never be destroyed. This is the reason that amidst their continual wars, and the losses all the nations of Europe suffer from each other, they are almost all thriving. And if I may indulge a conjecture, it may be one among several of the causes that have reduced the trade of Holland, that since the treaty of Utrecht, now above forty years, they have had no war. They may, during the quarrels of other powers, appear to have derived great advantages from their neutrality. But are they not with all this declining fast? And is not this country, which grew to be a nation, and to be a powerful trading and rich nation, in the midſt of the moſt bloody and expenſive wars, now loſing its trade, its riches, and its power, and almoſt ceaſing to be a nation, in the midſt of a profound peace of upwards of forty years. We muſt not forget, what the great Colbert ſaid of his country, and which we have experienced to be true, that the induſtry of the French if permitted would turn the very rocks into gold. We muſt not therefore place our dependence for keeping ourſelves on a par of power with France, upon the prejudice which we can do its trade in time of war, but upon the vigour, œconomy, and wiſdom of the meaſures which we take to ſecure and advance our own, both in war and in peace.

The largeſt town in the French part of Hiſpaniola is Cape Francoiſe, which is ſituated on the Northern part of the iſland upon a very fine harbour. It is well built, and contains about eight thouſand inhabitants blacks and whites: But tho' this be the largeſt town, Leogane on the Weſtern ſide, a good port too, and a place of conſiderable trade, is the ſeat of government, which here reſides in the hands of a governor and the intendant, who are mutually a check upon each other. There are beſides two other towns, conſiderable for their trade, Petit Guaves on the Weſt end of the iſland, and Port Loüis on the South-Weſt part.

C H A P.

CHAP. III.

A description of Martinico. Of Guardaloupe and other French islands. Their produce. Observations on the mistakes that have been made about their value.

Martinico is the next island in importance, which the French possess in America. It is one of the Caribbees or Windward islands, and the principal of them; about sixty miles in length, and at a medium about half as much in breadth. It is forty leagues to the North-West of Barbadoes. It has pretty high hills, especially in the inland parts. From those hills are poured out upon every side a number of agreeable and useful rivulets, which adorn and fructify this island in a high degree. The bays and harbours are numerous, safe and commodious; and so well fortified, that we have always failed in our attempts upon this place. The soil is fruitful enough, abounding in the same things which our islands in that part of the world produce, and upon which I shall the less insist on that account. Sugar is here, as it is in all the islands, the principal commodity, and great quantities are here made. Their export cannot be less than sixty or seventy thousand hogsheads, of five or six hundred weight, annually, and this certainly is no extravagant eſtimation. Indigo, cotton, piemento or allſpice, ginger, and aloes, are raiſed here; and coffee in great abundance; but to what value I cannot exactly ſay. Martinico is the reſidence of the governor of the French iſlands in theſe ſeas.

Guardaloupe is the largeſt of all the Caribbees, and in that diviſion called the Leeward iſlands. It is almoſt cut in two by a deep gulph that cloſes the ſides of a narrow iſthmus, which connects the two peninſulas that compoſe this iſland. It is upwards of ſixty miles long, and about the ſame breadth. Its ſoil is not inferior to that of Martinico; it is equally cultivated; and it is fortified with equal ſtrength; its produce is the ſame with that of Martinico; its export of ſugar is as great, beſides indigo, cotton, and thoſe other commodities, which are produced in all the iſlands of that part of America called the Weſt-Indies.

The reſt of the French iſlands in thoſe ſeas are Deſiada, St. Bartholomew, and Marigalante; all of them inconſiderable in compariſon of thoſe which we have mentioned. They do not all together produce above ſeven or eight thouſand hogſheads of ſugar. As for the iſland of St. Vincent, it is in the poſſeſſion of the native Americans, and of runaway negroes from the reſt of the Caribbees. The French maintain them in this poſſeſſion. Santa Lucia,

Lucia, or as it is often called, Sant Alouzie, of which the French are themselves in possession, and have settled, contrary to the faith of treaties, it is impossible to say any thing of its produce; it has been so newly planted, that it cannot as yet yield a great deal, and it is, even in our present circumstances, much our fault if it ever yields a great deal to France. These islands, besides their staple commodities, send home rocou, and brazil wood, in considerable quantities for the use of dyers; cassia for the druggists, and rosewood for joiners. The French have a settlement upon an island on the coast of Terra Firma in the province of Guiana, which they call Caen; and they claim besides a considerable part of the adjacent continent, but they have not much extended their settlements that way. The island is excessively unhealthy, though not so bad as formerly. The French here raise the same commodities which they have from the Caribbee islands, and in no inconsiderable quantity.

In estimating the produce of these islands, it is not in my power to be very exact. I have made the best inquiries I could, and principally took care not to exaggerate. I have, indeed, made the produce of the Caribbee islands very much greater than the ingenious collector of Harris's voyages; but then I am the less fearful of differing from him, as he seems a little to differ from himself, and not to have considered this point with his usual attention; for of Martinico he says, "That as it is larger, so it has many more inhabitants than Barbadoes, and produces more sugars, &c." And speaking of Guardaloupe a little lower, he observes, "That it produces more sugars than any of the British islands, except Jamaica;" and yet afterwards coming to sum up the products of all these islands, he allows but fifteen thousand hogsheads of sugar, of about six hundred weight each, for the whole; when he makes the single island of Barbadoes to yeild double the quantity of sugars which Martinico, Guardaloupe, and all the French Caribbees put together produce. For he rates it in the year 1730, at twenty-two thousand hogsheads, and upwards, of thirteen hundred weight. He must therefore certainly have made some mistake, excusable enough in so vast a work, which is executed in general in a very masterly manner.

On the whole, from the best informations I can get, the French at present greatly exceed our islands in the quantity of sugars which they produce; and it is as certain, that they are far less on the decline in that trade than we are, at least as things stood before the war; that they cultivate great quantities of indigo; a trade which our colonies in the West-Indies have entirely

entirely loſt; that within theſe few years they have ſent to Europe abundance of coffee, which our iſlands have not ſufficient encouragement to raiſe; and that upon the whole, we have the greateſt reaſon to be jealous of France in that part of the world. What advantages they derive from the noble iſland of Hiſpaniola we have ſeen. What muſt they do, if they come to poſſeſs the whole of that iſland, which in the cutting and ſhuffling of a treaty of peace is no way impoſſible? We ſhall then change the indolent Spaniard for the neighbourhood of the lively, vigilant, and enterpriſing French. And what a rivalry in peace, and what a danger in war that neighbourhood is even now, and much more will probably be, is but too apparent. Jamaica is near it; and for ſo valuable a poſſeſſion in ſo dangerous a ſituation, perhaps not ſo well defended. If beſides this, the French ſhould retain the iſlands of St. Vincent, St. Lucia, and Tobago, though they ſhould only turn them into Plantations for fire wood, lumber, and proviſions, as in ſuch a caſe it would ſeem moſt adviſeable to do with ſome of them at leaſt, what an advantage to their colonies! what an annoyance to ours! which they in a manner ſurround, and can in a ſort hold beſieged by the private armaments they may from thence fit out.

Theſe laſt mentioned iſlands were left neutral at the laſt peace; or in other words, they were

left at the extinction of the old, in juft the order proper for kindling a new flame (though fuch a defign, I am convinced, was far from the intentions of one of the parties) and in all refpects as if things were exprefsly ordered for that very purpofe. Indeed nothing can be attended with worfe confequences than thefe political after-reckonings, which the party who has the advantage at making the peace, never finds it his account to fettle or adjuft; but there they lie, full of matter of litigation; full of idle occafions for formal bufinefs; full of ftrife, and of ill blood; and, when a proper time occurs, of bloody and expenfive wars. It were better, at any rate, all at once to know what we are to depend upon; the beft or the worft we have to expect. If on the conclufion of a peace, things fhould take for us fuch an unfortunate turn, we have ftill great refources in the territories we poffefs. Jamaica is nothing like fully cultivated. The Bahamas, our undifputed right, where it is highly probable fugars might be cultivated to advantage, remain at prefent utterly neglected, as if unworthy of all notice, though they are many in number, large in extent, fruitful in their foil, fituated in a very happy climate, and are in a manner the keys of the Weft-India navigation. But we fhall pafs by all reflections on this fubject for the prefent, to look at the poffeffions and claims of France upon
the

the continent, which, if they were as well cultivated as they are fruitful and extensive, or as convenient objects of the French industry as their islands, they would, I make no doubt, be at least as advantageous to the trade, and add as much to the wealth and power of that flourishing kingdom.

CHAP. IV.

French North America. Description of Canada. Its climate. The fair of Mont-Real. Quebec. The inhabitants of Canada. The river St. Laurence and the great lakes. Cape Breton.

THE French possessions and claims in North America consist of an immense inland country, communicating with the sea by the mouths of two great rivers; both of difficult and dangerous navigation at the entrance; and one of which is quite frozen for almost half the year, and covered with thick exhalations and fogs for the greater part of the rest. They divide this vast country, which has our colonies on the East and North-East; the Spanish on the South-West and South-East; and to the Westward that unknown tract of land which stretches to the South-Sea; into two great provinces; the Northern of which they call Canada, and the
Southern

Southern Louisiana. But how far the bounds of these countries, extended to dimensions almost as great as all Europe, by the ambition of France, ought to be contracted by the rights of other powers, I shall not undertake to determine; as after all, such questions must be decided in a manner altogether different from any thing that can be said here.

Canada, which borders upon our provinces of Nova-Scotia, New-England, and New-York, is of a climate not altogether different from theirs; but as it is much further from the sea, and more Northerly than a great part of those provinces, it has a much severer winter; though the air is generally clear. The soil is various; mostly barren; but the French have settlements where the land is equal in goodness to that in any of our colonies, and wants nothing but a better convenience of market to make it equally advantageous to the proprietors. It yields Indian corn very well in most parts, and very fine wheat in some. All sorts of garden stuff which grows in Europe flourishes here. But they raise no staple commodity to answer their demands upon Old France; their trade with the Indians produces all their returns for that market. They are the furs of the beaver principally, and those of foxes and racoons, with deer-skins, and all the branches of the peltry. These, with what corn and lumber they send to the West-Indies, to a people not very luxurious, nor extremely numerous, furnish though very little money, yet wherewithal in a plentiful country, to render life easy and agreeable.

The nature of the climate severely cold for the most part, and the people manufacturing nothing, shews what the country wants from Europe; wine, brandy, cloths, chiefly coarse, linen, and wrought iron. The Indian trade requires brandy, tobacco, a sort of duffil blankets, guns, powder and ball, kettles, hatchets, and tomahawks, with several toys and trinkets. The Indians supply the peltry, and the French have traders, whom they call coureurs de bois, who, in the manner of the original inhabitants, traversing the vast lakes and rivers that divide this country, in canoes of bark, with incredible industry and patience, carry their goods into the remotest parts of America, and amongst nations entirely unknown to us. This again brings the market home to them, as the Indians are hereby habituated to trade with them. For this purpose, people from all parts, even from the distance of a thousand miles, come to the French fair of Mont-Real, which is held in June. On this occasion many solemnities are observed; guards are placed, and the governor assists to preserve order in such a concourse of such a variety of savage nations. The trade is now in that channel, for though many,

many, if not moſt of theſe nations, actually paſs by our ſettlement of Albany in New-York, where they may have the goods they want cheaper conſiderably than at Mont-Real, they travel on above two hundred miles further, to buy the ſame commodities at the ſecond hand, and enhanced by the expence of ſo long a land cárriage, at the French fair. For the French find it cheaper to buy our goods from the New-York merchants than to have them from their own, after ſo bad and ſo tedious a paſſage as it is from the mouth of the river St. Laurence to Mont-Real. So much do the French exceed us in induſtry, œconomy, and the arts of conciliating the affections of mankind; things that even balance all the diſadvantages they naturally labour under in this country. Our fort of Oſwego was well planned for ſecuring the Indian trade, and actually brought us a great part of it. But it is now no longer an interruption to the French commerce.

Having mentioned Mont-Real, I have only to obſerve, that this town is ſituated in an iſland in the river St. Laurence. This iſland lies in a very favourable climate, and is well inhabited and well planted. The city, which is ſometimes called Mont-Real, ſometimes Ville Marie, is agreeably ſituated on a branch of the river St. Laurence; it forms an oblong ſquare, divided by regular and well-cut ſtreets;

it

Settlements in America.

it contains three convents; with handsome churches, and an hospital for the sick. The fortifications are pretty good. The inhabitants are said to be about five thousand. The river is only navigable hither by canoes, or small craft, having several falls between this town and Quebec. Yet the Indian fair, and the trade of the same kind, which they drive more or less for the whole year, make it no inconsiderable place.

Quebec, the capital, lies much nearer to the sea; from which, however, it is one hundred and fifty leagues distant. The river, which from the sea hither is ten or twelve miles broad, narrows all of a sudden to about a mile wide. The town is divided into an upper and a lower; the houses in both are of stone, and in a tolerable manner. The fortifications are strong, though not regular; but its situation on a rock, washed by the river St. Laurence, is its chief defence. The city is a bishopric; but the cathedral is mean, and unworthy the capital of New France. The episcopal palace is however a building of a good appearance. Here is likewise a college of Jesuits, not unelegant; two convents and two hospitals. The town is covered with a regular and beautiful citadel, in which the governor resides. This city, though the capital of Canada, is however not very large. It contains about seven or eight thousand inhabitants

bitants at the utmoft. Ships of the greateft burden load and unload here, and a good many are built.

From Quebec to Mont-Real, which is about one hundred and fifty miles diftance, the country on both fides the river is very well fettled, and has an agreeable effect upon the eye. The farms lie pretty clofe all the way; feveral gentlemen's houfes, neatly built, fhew themfelves at intervals; and there is all the appearance of a flourifhing colony; but there are no towns or villages. It is pretty much like the well-fettled parts of our colonies of Virginia and Maryland, where the planters are wholly within themfelves.

With all the attention of the court of France to the trade and peopling of this, as well as their other colonies on the continent, they have not been yet able thoroughly to overcome the confequences of thofe difficulties which the climate, whilft the place was unfettled, threw in their way; their loffes in the wars with that brave and fierce nation the Iroquois, who more than once reduced their colony to their laft extremity, and the bad navigation of the river St. Laurence, which is an evil incurable, have kept back the colony. Therefore, though it is the oldeft of all the French eftablifhments, and prior to our fettlement of New-England, the inhabitants are not above one hundred thoufand fouls. Some indeed

indeed of late reckon them but at forty thoufand. An error that is very prejudicial to our affairs, whilft we overvalued our own ftrength, and under-rated the force of the enemy, and acted in a good meafure in conformity to fuch ideas; but even this number, as I eftimate it, which I believe is not far from the reality, might be no juft caufe of dread to our colonies, if they managed the ftrength they have, and which is certainly much fuperior, with fkill and effect. The French from theirs, though inferior, have feven or eight thoufand militia, hardy and well difciplined, always in readinefs to co-operate with their regular troops; and there is nothing which may hinder or retard their operations from within themfelves. It is therefore not more the French intrigues and their intermarriages with the Indians, which fix that people in the French intereft, than the fuccours which they are always fure to have from fuch a force, ever in readinefs to protect them whilft they remain their freinds, or to punifh them whenever they dare to appear as enemies. With us the cafe is quite otherwife. This favage people commence hoftilities againft us without any previous notice, and often without any provocation, they commit the moft horrid ravages for a long time with impunity. But when at laft their barbarities have roufed the fleeping ftrength of our people, at the fame time too
that

that they have confiderably leffened it, they are not afhamed to beg a peace; they know we always grant it readily; they promife it fhall endure as long as the fun and moon; and then all is quiet, till the French intrigues, co-operating with our indolence, give them once more an opportunity of ravaging our colonies, and of once more renewing a peace to be broken like all the former.

The great river St. Laurence is that only upon which the French have fettlements of any note; but if we look forward into futurity, it is nothing improbable that this vaft country, whoever then fhall be the poffeffors of it, will be enabled of itfelf to carry on a vaft trade upon thefe great feas of frefh water which it environs. Here are five lakes, the fmalleft of which is a piece of fweet water greater than any in the other parts of the world; this is the lake Ontario, which is not lefs than two hundred leagues in circumference; Erie longer, but not fo broad, is about the fame extent. That of the Hurons fpreads greatly in width, and is in circumference not lefs than three hundred; as is that of Michigan, though like lake Erie, it is rather long and comparitively narrow. But the lake Superior, which contains feveral large iflands, is five hundred leagues in the circuit. All of thefe are navigable by any veffels, and they all communicate with one another, except

cept that the passage between Erie and Ontario is interrupted by the stupendous cataract of Niagara, where the water tumbles down a precipice of twenty-six fathom high, and makes in this fall a thundring noise, which is heard all round the country at the distance of several miles. The river St. Laurence is the outlet of these lakes; by this they discharge themselves into the ocean. The French have built forts at the several straits, by which these lakes communicate with each other, as well as where the last of them communicates with the river St. Laurence. By these they effectually secure to themselves the trade of the lakes, and an influence upon all the nations of Americans which confine upon them.

They have but one settlement more in the Northern part of their territories in America, which deserves consideration; but that settlement, though a small one, is perhaps of more consequence than all the rest. It is the island of Cape Breton. This island properly belongs to the division of Acadia or Nova-Scotia, and it is the only part of it which has not been ceded by treaty to Great Britain. It is about one hundred and forty miles in length, full of mountains and lakes, and intersected by a vast number of creeks and bays, almost meeting each other on every side; which seems in general both for the coast and inland, very much to resemble the coast and inland parts of most Northern countries. Scotland is so; so is Iceland; and Denmark and Sweden have such shores, such mountains, and such lakes. However, the soil is in many places sufficiently fruitful; and in every part abounds with timber fit for all uses. In the earth are coal-pits; and on the shores one of the most valuable fisheries in the world. The only town in this island is Louisbourg. It stands upon one of the finest harbours in all America. This harbour is four leagues in circumference, landlocked every way but at the mouth, which is narrow; and within there is fine anchorage every where in seven fathom water. The town itself is of a tolerable size, and well built and fortified. The harbour is defended by batteries of cannon and forts, which secure it at this day, perhaps too effectually. This harbour is open the whole year. The French ships that carry goods to Quebec can very seldom get their full loading there, therefore on their return they put into Louisbourg, and there take in a quantity of fish, coal, and some lumber, and then sail away to the French islands in the West-Indies, where they vend these, and soon compleat their cargo with sugars. It is needless to observe that this island was taken by us in the late war, but restored by the treaty of Aix la Chapelle, in which we certainly were not in such a condition as to entitle us to prescribe the terms.

CHAP.

CHAP. V.

Louisiana. The Mississippi. The Ohio. The fountain of youth. The colony of Louisiana.

THE French have called the South part of the vast tract which they claim in America, Louisiana. It was heretofore a part of Florida. It is bounded by the gulph of Mexico upon the South. But what bounds it is to have to the East and to the West, it is to be wished the next treaty of peace may settle definitively. This is in all respects a much finer country than Canada; in a delicious climate, capable of bearing almost any thing from the tempter of the sky, and the goodness of the soil, and from the multitude of long, deep, and beautiful rivers, with which it is every where enriched and adorned; these are most of them navigable for hundreds of miles into the country. They are principally the Mississippi, whose head is unknown, but it almost goes quite through North America, and at certain seasons overflows its banks for a vast way on both sides. The Ohio, a river almost equal to the Danube, which falls into the Mississippi; the Ouabache, scarce inferior to the Ohio; the great rivers, Alibama, Mobile, and several others. The face of the country is almoſt wholly plain, covered with ſtately woods, or ſpread into very fine meadows. In ſhort, Louiſiana, particularly the Northern part, (for the mouth of the Miſſiſippi is barren) without any of theſe heightenings which it received, when it was made the inſtrument to captivate ſo many to their ruin, is in all reſpects a moſt deſirable place, though there be no ſufficient reaſons to believe that it contains any rich metals, which gave it the greateſt influence in that remarkable deluſion in 1717.

I know not how it has happened, but it has been the fate of this country to create romantic ideas at all times. Very ſurpriſing ſtories were told of it when firſt the Spaniards diſcovered the Weſt-India iſlands. Amongſt others, a notion was generally current, that there was a fountain here which perpetually renewed the youth of thoſe who drank it. This was ſo uniformly and confidently affirmed, that Juan Pontio de Leon, a conſiderable man among the Spaniſh adventurers, gave credit to it, and made a particular expedition for the diſcovery of that fairy land, and that fountain of youth. He was the firſt of the Europeans who landed in Florida. But what ſucceſs ſoever he met with in ſearch for that celebrated ſpring, it is certain he died not long after, having ſearched every part of the country, and drank of almoſt every water it contained.

contained. Nor do I find that so invaluable a spring is yet discovered there; if it were, it would undoubtedly be the best commodity the country could yield, both for domestic consumption, and for the foreign markets, and would be a far better basis for stocks and funds than the richest mines of gold or silver. Yet, without this, an idea, altogether as romantic, of a trade hither, opperated so strongly upon a very wise nation, as to serve for the instrument of one of those dangerous masterstrokes in politics, by which nations are sometimes saved, individuals undone, and an entire change and reversement brought about, not only in the common ways of thinking of mankind, but of all that seemed most fixed and permanent in a state. The famous Mississippi scheme in France was of that nature, and built upon such a romantic foundation. It is well known to all the world, both on its own account, and upon account of a similar madness that prevailed here, without perhaps being attended with such advantageous consequences.

The French settled in Louisiana raise some indigo, a good deal of cotton, some corn and rice, with lumber for their islands; but the colony is not very vigorous, on account of the shoals and sands with which the mouth of the river Mississippi is in a manner choaked up, and which deny access to vessels of any considerable

considerable burden. This keeps the inhabitants low; but the cause which keeps them from growing rich contributes too to their security; for it is not easy to act with any great force upon that side. But the French have not relied upon this advantage; but according to their usual cautions and wise custom, have erected several forts in the most material places, and fortified, as it is said, New Orleans their capital, and indeed the only city in Louisiana, in a regular manner. This city is not remarkably fair, large, or rich; but it is laid out regularly, in a fine situation on the banks of the Missisippi, in prospect of an higher fortune. The whole colony is said not to contain above ten thousand souls, whites and negroes. Yet with all its disadvantages, this colony is not declining; and if ever they should make the mouth of the Missisippi more tractable; (and what is impossible to ambition and industry?) if they should come fully to possess and settle the Ohio, which at one season overflows, and makes such flood as to level all the falls almost from its very source to the mouth of the Missisippi, and gives a passage all that way to very considerable vessels, (though they have not quite the same easy return); and if by this and other means they should contrive a communication between Canada and the settlement at Louisiana, whilst they entirely confine us between our mountains and the sea,

Louisiana in a few years will wear quite another face. It will supply their West-Indies with boards, staves, horses mules, and provisions. It will send tobacco into France; and increasing the conveniencies of its mother country, and sister colonies, it will increase its own traffic, its inhabitants, and its power. But the French not trusting to this remote prospect, have established themselves at the mouth of the Mobile; a river which falls into the gulph of Mexico. And many are of opinion that this is a more advantageous situation, not only for the maritime but for the inland commerce, and the communication of their colonies, than the Missisippi. It certainly approaches much nearer to our settlements, and whilst it serves the French better, is much better calculated to annoy our Southern colonies. We have seen how the French West-Indies in less than forty years, from a condition which could excite no other sentiments than those of compassion, are risen to such a pitch as to be an object of great and just terror to her neighbours; and we now feel too, that the French settlements in North America, even such as they are, are not an undermatch for the whole force of ours, in the manner at least in which that force is exerted.

CHAP. VI.

The French policy with regard to their colonies.

THAT we may not sit down in a senseless admiration of this progress of the French colonies, as if it were the work of fortune, it will not be amiss to open something of the wise plan of conduct which France has pursued with regard to this interesting object. They are sensible, as the mother country is to receive ultimately all the benefits of their labours and acquisitions, so that all the prosperity of their plantations must be derived from the attention with which they are regarded at home. For which reason the plantations are particularly under the care and inspection of the council of commerce; a board very judiciously constituted to answer the purposes for which it is designed. To give it a proper respect and authority, it is composed of twelve of the most considerable officers of the crown; and then to enable it to judge perfectly of the matters which come before it, these twelve are assisted by the deputies of all the considerable trading towns and cities in France, who are chosen out of the richest and most intelligent of their traders, and paid an handsome salary for their attendance at Paris, from the funds of their respective cities. This council sits once a week. The deputies propose plans for redressing every grievance in trade; for raising the branches that are fallen; for extending new ones; for supporting the old; and in fine, for every thing that may improve the working, or promote the vent of their manufactures, according to their own lights, or to the instructions of their constituents. They have a watchful eye upon every article of commerce; and they not only propose helps and improvements to it themselves, but they hear the proposals of others, which are not disdainfully rejected, nor rashly received. They do not render the access to them difficult, by swelling themselves into a stiff and unwieldly state. They do not discourage those who apply, by admitting the vexatious practice of fees, perquisites, and exactions, in their inferior officers. They do not suffer form and methods to load and encumber that business, they were solely intended to advance. They summon and examine those who are supposed the most competent judges of the matter before them, and of every part of it, even the lowest artizans: but though they examine those men, they are instructed by their experience, not determined by their opinion. When they are satisfied of the usefulness of any regulation, they propose it to the royal council, where their report is always

ways received with particular attention. An edict to enforce it issues accordingly; and it is executed with a punctuality which distinguishes their government, and which alone can make the wisest regulations any thing better than serious mockeries. To the care of this excellent body the plantations are particularly entrusted.

The government of the several divisions of their colonies is in a governor, an intendant, and a royal council. The governor is invested with a great deal of power; which however, on the side of the crown, is checked by the intendant, who has the care of the king's rights, and whatever relates to the revenue; and on the side of the people, it is checked by the royal council, whose office it is, to see that the people are not oppressed by the one, nor defrauded by the other; and they are all checked by the constant and jealous eye which the government at home keeps over them. For the officers at all the ports of France are charged under the severest penalties, to interrogate all captains of ships coming from the colonies concerning the reception they met at the ports they were bound to; how justice was administered to them? what charges they were made liable to, and of what kinds? The passengers, and even the sailors are examined upon these heads, and a verbal process of the whole is formed and
trans-

transmitted with all speed to the admiralty. Complaints are encouraged; but a difference is made between hearing an accusation and condemning upon it.

That the colonies may have as little load as possible, and that the governor may have less temptation to stir up troublesome intrigues, or favour factions in his government, his salary is paid by the crown. His perquisites are none; and he is strictly forbidden to carry on any trade, or to have any plantations in the islands, or on the continent, or any interest whatever in goods or lands within his government, except the house he lives in, and a garden for his convenience and recreation. All the other officers are paid by the crown, and out of the revenues of Old France; the fortifications are built and repaired, and the soldiers are paid out of the same funds.

In general the colonies pay no taxes; but when upon an extraordinary emergency taxes have been raised, they were very moderate. And, that even the taxes might operate for the advancement of the colony, they who began new plantations, were exempted from them. The duties upon the export of their produce at the islands, or at its import into France, is next to nothing; in both places hardly making two per cent. What commodities go to them, pay no duties at all.

Besides

Besides these advantages, a considerable benefit accrues to such of the colonies as are poor, as Canada, by the money which comes from France to support the establishment. This brings into Canada about 120,000 crowns a year, which finds them circulating cash; preserves them from the dangerous expedient of a paper currency; enables them to keep up their intercourse with some credit, with their mother country; and at the same time is in fact no loss at all to it, since the money returns home almost as soon as it can possibly be transported back again.

In all their islands, judges of the admiralty are appointed to decide in a summary manner all disputes between merchants, and whatsoever else has any relation to trade. These judges are strictly examined before they are appointed, particularly as to their skill in the marine laws, which have been improved and digested in France with so much care and good sense, that all law-suits are quickly over; though in other respects the practice of law admits of as much chicanery, and has as many, if not more delays, than with us.

After having taken such precautions to secure the good government of the colony within itself, and to make its communication with the mother country easy and beneficial to both sides, all would be to very little purpose, if they had not provided with equal care to

have

have the country replenished with people. To answer this end, they oblige every ship which departs from France for America, to carry a certain number of indented servants. All vessels of sixty tuns or under are to carry three; from sixty to a hundred, four; and from a hundred upwards, six servants; sound strong bodies, between the ages of eighteen and forty. Before their departure, the servants are examined by the officers of the admiralty, to see whether they are the persons required by law; an examination to the same purpose is made by the commissary on their landing in America. They are to serve three years. The avarice of the planters makes them always prefer negroe slaves, because they are more obedient than the Europeans; may be more worked, are subsisted with less difficulty, and are besides the entire property of their master. This disposition, in time, would render the safety of the colony extremely precarious, whilst it made the colony itself of less value to the mother country. Therefore the planters are by law obliged to keep a certain number of white servants in proportion to their blacks; and the execution of this law is inforced by the commissary, who adjusts the price, and forces the planters to take the number of servants required by the ordinance, who would otherwise be a burden upon the hands of the masters of ships who brought them over.

They

They confider the planter, as a Frenchman venturing his life, enduring a fpecies of banifhment, and undergoing great hardfhips for the benefit of his country. For which reafons, he has great indulgence fhewn him. Whenever by hurricanes, earthquakes, or bad feafons, the planters fuffer, a ftop is put to the rigour of exacting creditors; the few taxes which are levied, are remitted; and even money is advanced to repair their loffes and fet them forward. To thofe who are poor, but fhew a difpofition to induftry, neceffaries and fmall fums are lent, to make a beginning; and this money is taken in gradually, and by very fmall payments. On the other hand, as it can be of no advantage to the planter to run fraudulently into debt, but that it is of the greateft prejudice to the French merchant, all debts, though contracted by the planters in France, are levied with great eafe. The procefs, properly authenticated, is tranfmitted to America, and admitted as proved there, and levied on the planter's eftate, of whatfoever kind it may be. However, care is taken, that whilft compulfory methods are ufed to make the planter do juftice, the ftate fhall not lofe the induftry of an ufeful member of the community; the debt is always levied according to the fubftance of the debtor, and by inftallments; fo that (what ought indeed to be the cafe in every well-regulated government) one of the parties is not facrificed to the other. Both

Both subsist; the creditor is satisfied; the debtor is not ruined; and the credit of the colonies is kept in health and vigour at home, by the sure methods which are in use for recovering all demands in the plantations.

As to the negroes, they are not left as they are with us, wholly, body and soul to the discretion of the planter. Their masters are obliged to have them instructed in the principles of religion. There are methods taken at once to protect the slaves from the cruelty of their owners, and to preserve the colony from the ill effects, that might arise from treating them with a lenity not consistent with their condition. In short, the Code Noir, and other ordinances relative to these poor creatures, shew a very just and sensible mixture of humanity and steadiness. There is however one error, their planters commit in common with ours; which is, that they overwork these unhappy men in a manner not suitable to the nature of the climate, or to their constitutions.

I have dwelt the longer upon the French policy as it regards their colonies, because it is just to give due honour to all those, who advance the intercourse of mankind, the peopling of the earth, and the advantage of their country by wise and effectual regulations. But I principally insist upon it, that it may, if possible,

sible, serve for an example to ourselves; that it may excite an emulation in us; that it may help to rouse us out of that languor into which we seem to be fallen. The war we now carry on, principally regards our colonies, and is a sufficient proof that we are come at last to know their value. But if we are not to hope for better success than has hitherto attended a very just cause, the next peace will probably contract the field we hoped to lay open to our industry in America. But we ought therefore to cultivate what still remains of it, with tenfold industry; we ought to guard with the most unremitting vigilance that enclosed spring, that sealed fountain, the waters of which we reserve to ourselves, and direct into such channels, and make to pursue such windings and turnings as best serve our purposes. We have, I believe, pretty well discovered most of our errors, and the advantage our enemy and rival has taken, not only of our supineness, but of a contrary genius in his own councils. We ought to rouse ourselves from the former, and prepare to imitate the latter. Our business is to fight against Alexander, not to rail at him. And truly, I do not know any thing, that for this long time past has contributed more to degrade our character for humanity in the eyes of foreigners, or to instil into ourselves a low and illiberal way of thinking

thinking, than that vein of licentious scurrility and abuse, by which, in all sorts of writings, we are apt to vilify and traduce the French nation. There is nothing, which hinders people from acting properly, more than indulging themselves in a vain and effeminate licence of tongue. A man who loves his country, and can at once oppose, and esteem an enemy, would view our present circumstances in a light, I conceive, somewhat like the following. We have been engaged for above a century with France in a noble contention for the superiority in arms, in politics, in learning, and in commerce; and there never was a time, perhaps, when this struggle was more critical. If we succeed in the war, even our success, unless managed with prudence, will be like some former successes, of little benefit to us; if we should fail, which God forbid, even then, prudence may make our misfortunes of more use to us, than an ill-managed success; if they teach us to avoid our former errors; if they make us less careless; if they make us cultivate the advantages we have with care and judgment: this, and not our opinion of the enemy, must decide the long contest between us.

CHAP. VII.

The Dutch settlements. Curassou. The city, its trade. The Spanish counterband. Eustatia. The Danish company. The Danish island of Santa Cruz. The characters of the several European nations as they regard America.

AFTER the Portuguese had dispossessed the Dutch of Brazil in the manner we have seen; and after the treaty of Nimeguen had entirely removed them out of North America, they were obliged to console themselves with their rich possessions in the East-Indies, and to sit down content in the West with Surinam; a country on the North-East part of South America, of no great value whilst we had it, and which we ceded to them in exchange for New-York; and with two or three small and barren islands in the North-sea not far from the Spanish main. The former of these, they are far from neglecting; they raise some sugar in Surinam; a great deal of cotton; coffee of an excellent kind, and some valuable dying drugs. They trade with our North American colonies, who bring hither horses, live cattle and provisions, and take home a large quantity of molasses; but their negroes are only the refuse

refuse of those they have for the Spanish market; and the Indians in their neighbourhood are their mortal enemies. On the same continent they have three other settlements at no considerable distance from each other, Boron, Berbice, and Approwack; none very great, but producing the same commodities with Surinam.

The islands which they possess are four, Curassou, St. Eustatia, Aruba and Bonaire; none of them large or fertile, but turned to the best advantage possible by that spirit of industry for which the Dutch are justly famous. Curacco or Curassou, as it is generally called, is about thirty miles long, and ten in breadth. Though it is naturally barren it produces a considerable quantity both of sugar and tobacco, and here are besides very great salt works, which furnish a good deal to the English islands, and for which there is a considerable demand from our colonies on the continent; but the trade for which this island is chiefly valuable, is that which in time of war is carried on between them, the English, and the French; and the counterband which is carried on between them and the Spaniards at all times.

The Dutch vessels from Europe touch at this island for intelligence or proper pilots, and then proceed to the Spanish coast upon a trade which they force with a strong hand.

It is very difficult for the Spanish guarda coftas to take these vessels; for they are not only stout ships with a number of guns; but by a very wise policy manned with a large crew of chosen seamen, who are all deeply interested in the safety of the vessel and the success of the voyage. They have each a share in the cargo of a value proportioned to the owner's station, supplied by the merchants upon credit, and at prime cost. This animates them with an uncommon courage; they fight bravely, because every man fights in defence of his own property. But there is besides this, a constant intercourse between the Spanish continent and this island.

The island of Curassou has its numerous warehouses always full of the commodities of Europe, and the East-Indies. Here are all sorts of woollen and linen cloths, laces, silks, ribbands, utensils of iron, naval and military stores, brandy, the spices of the Moluccas, and the callicoes of India, white and painted. Hither the West-India, which is likewise their African company, bring three or four cargoes of slaves annually. To this mart, the Spaniards come themselves in small vessels, and carry off not only the best of their negroes, and at the best price, but very great quantities of all sorts of goods I have mentioned; with this advantage to the seller, that the refuse of warehouses and

and mercers shops, things grown utterly unfashionable and unsaleable in Europe, go off extremely well, where every thing is sufficiently recommended by being European. They leave here their gold and silver in bars or coined, cacao, vanilla, cochineal, jesuit's bark, hides, and other valuable commodities. The ships that trade directly from Holland to the Spanish continent, as they touch here on their outward passage to gain intelligence or assistance, on their return put in here likewise to compleat what is wanting of their cargo, with the sugar, the tobacco, the ginger, and other produce of the island itself. The trade of this island, even in times of peace, is reputed to be worth to the Dutch, no less than 500,000l. sterling annually, but in time of war the profit is far greater, for then it is in a manner the common emporium of the West-Indies; it affords a great retreat to the ships of all nations, and at the same time refuses to none of them arms and ammunition to annoy one another. The intercourse with Spain being interrupted, the Spanish colonies have scarce any other market, from whence they can be well supplied either with slaves or goods; the French come hither to buy the beef, pork, corn, flour and lumber, which the English bring from the continent of North America, or which is transported from Ireland; so that whether in peace, or in war, the trade of this island flourishes extremely. Nor is this owing to any natural advantage whatsoever. It seems as if it were fated, that the ingenuity and patience of the Hollanders should every where, both in Europe and America, be employed in fighting against an unfriendly nature: for the island is not only barren, and dependent upon the rains for its water, but the harbour is naturally one of the worst in America; but the Dutch have entirely remedied that defect; they have upon this harbour one of the largest, and by far the most elegant and cleanly towns in the American islands. The public buildings are numerous and handsome; the private houses commodious; and the magazines large, convenient, and well filled. All kind of labour is here performed by engines; some of them so dexterously contrived, that ships are at once lifted into the dock, where they are compleatly careened; and then furnished with naval stores, provisions, cannon, and every thing requisite either for trade or war.

Eustatia is but one mountain of about twenty miles in compass; it is amongst the Leeward Islands; but though so small and inconveniently laid out by nature, the industry of the Dutch have made it turn out to very good account, and it is fully peopled; the sides of the mountain are divided and
laid

laid out in very pretty settlements; and though they have neither springs nor rivers, they are so careful that they never want proper supplies of water from their ponds and cisterns. They raise here sugar and tobacco; and this island, as well as Curassou, is engaged in the Spanish counterband trade, for which, however, it is not so well situated; and it draws the same advantages from its constant neutrality.

As for Aruba and Bonaire; they lie near Curassou, and have no trade of consequence; they are chiefly employed in raising fresh provisions for the principal island, and for the refreshment of such ships as use these seas.

The trade of all the Dutch American settlements was originally carried on by the West-India company only. At present such ships as go upon that trade pay two and a half per cent. for their licences; the company however reserves to itself, the whole of what is carried on between Africa and the American islands.

The Danes had likewise a West-India company, though its object was far from extensive. It was little more than the island of St. Thomas, an inconsiderable member of the Caribbees; lately they have added to their possessions the island of Santa Cruz in the same cluster. These islands, so long as they

they remained in the hands of the company, were ill managed, and nothing like the proper advantage was made of them; but the present king of Denmark, inferior to none who ever sat upon that or any other throne, in love to his subjects, and a judicious zeal for promoting their welfare, has bought up that company's stock, and laid the trade open. Since then, the old settlement at St. Thomas is very much improved; it produces upwards of three thousand hogsheads of sugar at a thousand weight each, and others of the West-Indian commodities in tolerable plenty; and as for Santa Cruz, from a perfect desart a few years since, it is beginning to settle fast; several persons from the English islands, and amongst them some of great wealth, have gone to settle there, and have received very great encouragement to do so. The air of the place is extremely unhealthful, but this ill disposition will probably continue no longer than the woods, with which the island at present is almost wholly covered. These two nations, the Dutch and Danes, hardly deserve to be mentioned amongst the proprietors of America; their possessions there are comparatively nothing. But as they appear extremely worthy of the attention of these powers, and as the share of the Dutch is worth to them at least six hundred thousand

pounds

pounds sterling a year, what must we think of our possessions? what attention do they not deserve from us? and what may not be made of them by that attention?

There seems to be a remarkable providence in the casting the parts, if I may use that expression, of the several European nations who act upon the stage of America. The Spaniard, proud, lazy and magnificent, has an ample walk in which to expatiate; a soft climate to indulge his love of ease; and a profusion of gold and silver to procure him all those luxuries his pride demands, but which his laziness would refuse him.

The Portuguese, naturally indigent at home, and enterprizing rather than industrious abroad, has gold and diamonds as the Spaniard has, wants them as he does, but possesses them in a more useful, though a less ostentatious manner.

The English, of a reasoning disposition, thoughtful and cool, and men of business rather than of great industry, impatient of much fruitless labour, abhorrent of constraint, and lovers of a country life, have a lot which indeed produces neither gold nor silver; but they have a large tract of a fine continent; a noble field for the exercise of agriculture, and sufficient to furnish their trade without laying them under great difficulties. Intolerant as they are of the most useful restraints,
their

their commerce flourishes from the freedom every man has of pursuing it according to his own ideas, and directing his life after his own fashion.

The French, active, lively, enterprizing, pliable and politic, and though changing their pursuits, always pursuing the present object with eagerness, are notwithstanding tractable and obedient to rules and laws which bridle these dispositions, and wind and turn them to proper courses. This people have a country, where more is to be effected by managing the people than by cultivating the ground; where a pedling commerce, that requires constant motion, flourishes more than agriculture or a regular traffic; where they have difficulties which keep them alert by struggling with them, and where their obedience to a wise government serves them for personal wisdom. In the islands the whole is the work of their policy, and a right turn their government has taken.

The Dutch have got a rock or two on which to display the miracles of frugality and diligence, (which are their virtues,) and on which they have exerted these virtues, and shewn those miracles.

PART

PART VI.

The English Settlements.

CHAP. I.

The division of the English West-Indies. Description of Jamaica. Conquest of that island.

THE English colonies are the fairest objects of our attention in America, not only as they comprehend a vast and delightful variety of climates, situations, natural products, and improvements of art; but as they contain, though the dominions of one potentate, and their inhabitants formed out of the people of one nation, an almost equal variety of manners, religions and ways of living. They have a most flourishing trade with their mother country, and they communicate widely with many foreign nations; for besides the constant and

and useful intercourse they hold with Africa, their ships are seen in the ports of Spain, Portugal, Italy, and even in the Levant; nor are they excluded the American settlements of France, Spain, Portugal and Holland. This, with their constant correspondence with each other, and with their mother country, hurries about a lively circulation of trade, of which Great Britain is the heart and spring, from whence it takes its rise, and to which it all returns in the end.

In some of the European settlements we have seen the effects of a vast ambition supported by surprizing feats of a romantic courage mixed with an insatiable thirst of gold. In others, the regular product of a systematic policy tempering and guiding an active industry; but in our own colonies we are to display the effects of liberty; the work of a people guided by their own genius, and following the directions of their own natural temper in a proper path.

I intend to consider the English colonies under two principal divisions; the first I allot to those islands which lie under the torrid zone between the tropic of Cancer and the Equinoctial line, in that part generally called the West-Indies. The second is to comprehend our possessions in the temperate zone on the continent of North America.

rica. The West-India islands shall be considered, as they are amongst the Greater Antilles; the Windward; or the Leeward islands. Amongst the first we possess the large and noble island of Jamaica; amongst the second we have Barbadoes; and in the third St. Christopher's, Antegua, Nevis, Montserrat, and Barbuda. As all these islands lie between the tropics, whatever is to be said of the air, winds, meteors, and natural produce, shall fall under one head, as they are the same or nearly the same in all of them; their produce for the market is nearly the same too; and therefore whatever is to be said of the manufacturing of those, shall come together, after we have given a concise description of the state of each island separately.

Jamaica lies between the 75th and 79th degrees of West longitude from London, and is between seventeen and nineteen degrees distant from the Equinoctial. It is in length, from East to West, a hundred and forty English miles; in breadth about sixty; and of an oval form. This country is in a manner intersected with a ridge of lofty mountains, rugged and rocky, that are called the blue mountains. On each side of the blue mountains are chains of lesser mountains gradually lower. The greater mountains are little better than so many rocks; where

where there is any earth, it is only a stubborn clay fit for no sort of husbandry. The mountains are very steep, and the rocks tumbled upon one another in a manner altogether stupendous, the effect of the frequent earthquakes which have shaken this island in all times. Yet barren as these mountains are, they are all covered to the very top with a great variety of beautiful trees, flourishing in a perpetual spring; their roots penetrate the crannies of the rocks, and search out the moisture which is lodged there by the rains that fall so frequently on these mountains, and the mists that almost perpetually brood upon them. These rocks too are the parents of a vast number of fine rivulets, which tumble down their sides in cataracts, that form amongst the rudeness of the rocks and precipices, and the shining verdure of the trees, the most wildly pleasing imagery imaginable. The face of this country is a good deal different from what is generally observed in other places. For as on one hand the mountains are very steep; so the plains between them are perfectly smooth and level. In these plains, the soil augmented by the wash of the mountains for so many ages, is prodigiously fertile. None of our islands produce so fine sugars. They formerly had here cacao in great perfection, which delights in a rich ground. Their pastures after the

rains,

rains, are of a most beautiful verdure, and extraordinary fatness. They are called Savannas. On the whole, if this island were not troubled with great thunders and lightnings, hurricanes, and earthquakes; and if the air was not at once violently hot, damp, and extremely unwholsome in most parts, the fertility and beauty of this country would make it as desirable a situation for pleasure, as it is for the profits, which in spite of these disadvantages draw hither such a number of people.

The river waters are many of them unwholsome and taste of copper; but some springs there are of a better kind. In the plains are found several salt fountains; and in the mountains, not far from Spanish-town, is a hot bath, of extraordinary medicinal virtues. It relieves in the dry belly-ach, one of the most terrible endemial distempers of Jamaica, and in various other complaints.

This island came into our possession during the usurpation of Cromwell, and by means of an armament which had another destination. Cromwell, notwithstanding the great abilities which enabled him to overturn the constitution, and to trample upon the liberties of his country, was not sufficiently acquainted with foreign politics. This ignorance made him connect himself closely
with

with France, then rising into a dangerous grandeur, and to fight with great animosity, the shadow which remained of the Spanish power. On such ideas he fitted out a formidable fleet, with a view to reduce the island of Hispaniola; and though he failed in this design, Jamaica made amends not only for this failure, but almost for the ill policy which first drew him into hostilities with the Spaniards; by which, however, he added this excellent country to the British dominions.

There was nothing of the genius of Cromwell to be seen in the planning of this expedition. From the first to the last all was wrong; all was a chain of little interested mismanagement, and had no air of the result of absolute power lodged in great hands. The fleet was ill victualled; the troops ill provided with necessaries to support and encourage men badly chosen and worse armed. They embarked in great discontent. The generals were but little better satisfied, and had little more hopes than the soldiers. But the generals, (for there were two in the command, Pen and Venables, one for the marine, the other for the land service,) were men of no extraordinary talents. And, if they had been men of the best capacity, little was to be expected from two commanders not subordinate, and so differing in their ideas,

ideas, and so envious of each other as land and sea-officers generally are. But to make this arrangement perfect in all respects, and to improve the advantages arising from a divided command, they added a number of commissioners as a check upon both. This tripartite generalship, in the truest Dutch taste, produced the effects that might be expected from it. The soldiers differed with the generals, the generals disagreed with one another, and all quarrelled with the commissioners. The place of their landing in Hispaniola was ill chosen, and the manner of it wretchedly contrived. The army had near forty miles to march before it could act; and the soldiers, without order, without heart, fainting and dying by the excessive heat of the climate and the want of necessary provisions, and disheartened yet more by the cowardice and discontent of their officers, yielded an easy victory to an handful of Spaniards. They retired ignominiously and with great loss.

But the principal commanders, a little reconciled by their misfortunes, and fearing to return to England without effect, very wisely turned their thoughts another way. They resolved to attempt Jamaica, before the inhabitants of that island could receive encouragement by the news of their defeat in Hispaniola. They knew that this island was in no good posture of defence; and they set themselves vigorously to avoid the mistakes, which proved so fatal in the former expedition. They severely punished the officers who had shewn an ill example by their cowardice; and they ordered with respect to the soldiers, that if any attempted to run away, the man nearest to him should shoot him.

Fortified with these regulations they landed in Jamaica, and laid siege to St. Jago de la Vega, now called Spanish-town, the capital of the island. The people, who were in no condition to oppose an army of ten thousand men, and a strong naval force, would have surrendered immediately, if they had not been encouraged by the strange delays of our generals and their commissioners. However at last the town with the whole island surrendered, but not until the inhabitants had secreted their most valuable effects in the mountains.

CHAP.

CHAP. II.

The settlement of Jamaica. The failure of cacao. The buccaneers. The flourishing state of that island. Its decline in some respects.

AFTER the restoration, the Spaniards ceded the island to our court. Cromwell had settled there some of the troops employed in its reduction; some royalists uneasy at home sought an asylum in this island; not a few planters from Barbadoes were invited to Jamaica by the extraordinary fertility of the soil, and the other advantages which it offered. These latter taught the former settlers the manner of raising the sugar cane, and making sugar. For at first they had wholly applied themselves to the raising of cacao, as the Spaniards had done before them. It was happy for them that they fell into this new practice; for the cacao groves planted by the Spaniards began to fail, and the new plantations did not answer, as the negroes foretold they would not, because of the want of certain religious ceremonies always used by the Spaniards in planting them, at which none of the slaves were suffered to be present, and to the use of which they attributed the prosperity of these plantations.

tions. Probably there were methods taken at that time, that were covered by the veil of these religious ceremonies, which are neceſſary to the well-being of that plant. However that be, the cacao has never ſince equalled the reputation of the Spaniſh, but gave way to the more profitable cultivation of Indigo and ſugar.

But what gave the greateſt life to this new ſettlement, and raiſed it at once to a ſurprizing pitch of opulence, which it hardly equals even in our days, was the reſort thither of thoſe pirates called the buccaneers. Theſe men who fought with the moſt deſperate bravery, and ſpent their plunder with the moſt ſtupid extravagance, were very welcome gueſts in Jamaica. They often brought two, three, and four hundred thouſand pieces of eight at a time, which were immediately ſquandered in all the ways of exceſſive gaming, wine and women. Vaſt fortunes were made, and the returns of treaſure to England were prodigiouſly great. In the iſland they had by this means raiſed ſuch funds, that when the ſource of this wealth was ſtopped up by the ſuppreſſion of the pirates, they were enabled to turn their induſtry into better channels. They increaſed ſo faſt, that it was computed that in the beginning of this century, they had ſixty thouſand whites and a hundred and

twenty

twenty thousand negroes in this island. This calculation is certainly too large. However, the Jamaicans were undoubtedly very numerous until reduced by earthquakes, (one of which entirely ruined Port-Royal, and killed a vast number of persons in all parts of the country) and by terrible epidemical diseases, which treading on the heels of the former calamities swept away vast multitudes. Losses which have not been since sufficiently repaired. At present the white inhabitants scarcely exceed twenty five thousand souls; the blacks are about ninety thousand; both much less numerous than formerly, and with a disproportion much greater on the side of the whites.

It appears at present, that Jamaica is rather upon the decline; a point this that deserves the most attentive consideration. A country which contains at least four millions of acres, has a fertile soil, an extensive sea coast, and many very fine harbours, for an island so circumstanced, and at a time when the value of all its products at market is considerably risen, for such a country to fall short of its former numbers, and not to have above three or four hundred thousand acres employed in any sort of culture, shews clearly that something must be very wrong in the management of its affairs; and what shews it even yet more clearly, land is so

extravagantly

extravagantly dear in many of the other iflands, as to fell fometimes for one hundred pounds an acre and upwards; a price that undoubtedly never would be paid, if convenient land was to be had, and proper encouragement given in Jamaica. Whether this be owing to public or private faults, I know not; but certain it is, that wherever they are, they deferve a fpeedy and effectual remedy from thofe, in whofe power it is to apply it.

CHAP. III.

The products of Jamaica. Piemento. Sugar. Rum. Molaffes. Cotton. Ginger. The logwood trade. Difputes about it. The counterband. Slave trade.

THE natural products of Jamaica, befides fugar, cacao, and ginger, are principally piemento, or, as it is called, allfpice, or Jamaica pepper. The tree which bears the piemento rifes to the height of above thirty feet. It is ftraight, of a moderate thicknefs, and covered with a grey bark extremely fmooth and fhining. It fhoots out a vaft number of branches upon all fides, that bear a plentiful foliage of very large and beautiful leaves of a fhining green, in all things refembling the leaf of the bay tree.

At

At the very end of the twigs are formed bunches of flowers; each ſtalk bearing a flower which bends back, and within which bend are to be diſcerned ſome ſtamina of a pale green colour; to theſe ſucceeds a bunch of ſmall crowned berries, larger when ripe than juniper berries; at that ſeaſon they change from their former green, and become black, ſmooth, and ſhining; they are taken unripe from the tree, and dried in the ſun; in this caſe they aſſume a brown colour, and have a mixed flavour of many kinds of ſpice, whence it is called allſpice. But it is milder than the other ſpices, and is judged to be inferior to none of them for the ſervice which it does to cold, watery and languid ſtomachs. The tree grows moſtly upon the mountains.

Beſides this, they have the wild cinamon tree, whoſe bark is ſo ſerviceable in medicine; the manchineel, a moſt beautiful tree to the eye, with the faireſt apple in the world, and when cut down affording a very fine ornamental wood for the joiners, but the apple, and the juice in every part of the tree, contain one of the worſt poiſons in nature. Here is the mahogany, in ſuch general uſe with our cabinet makers; the cabbage tree, a tall plant, famous for a ſubſtance, looking and taſting like cabbage, growing on the very top, and no leſs remarkable for the extreme hardneſs of its wood,

wood, which when dry is incorruptible, and hardly yields to any tool; the palma, from which is drawn a great deal of oil, much esteemed by the negroes both in food and medicine; the white wood, which never breeds the worm in ships; the soap tree, whose berries answer all purposes of washing; the mangrove and olive bark, useful to tanners; the fustic and redwood to the dyers, and lately the logwood; and their forests supply the apothecary with guaiacum, salsaparilla, china, cassia, and tamarinds; they have aloes too; and do not want the cochineal plant, though they know nothing of the art of managing it; nor perhaps is the climate suitable. The indigo plant was formerly much cultivated; the cotton tree is still so, and they send home more of its wool than all the rest of our islands together.

The whole product therefore of the island may be reduced to these heads. First sugars, of which they imported in 1753 twenty thousand three hundred and fifteen hogsheads, some vastly great even to a tun weight, which cannot be worth less in England than 424,725 pounds sterling. Most of this goes to London and Bristol, and some part of it to North America, in return for the beef, pork, cheese, corn, pease, staves, plank, pitch and tar, which they have from thence. 2. Rum, of which they export about

about 4000 puncheons. The rum of this island is generally esteemed the best, and is the most used in England. 3. Molasses, in which they make a great part of their returns for New England, where there are vast distilleries. All these are the produce of their grand staple the sugar cane. 4. Cotton, of which they send out 2000 bags. The indigo, formerly much cultivated, is now inconsiderable, but some cacao and coffee are exported, which latter is in no great esteem; though it is said to be little inferior to that of Mocha, provided it be kept for two or three years. With these they send home a considerable quantity of piemento, ginger, drugs for dyers and apothecaries, sweetmeats, and mahogany and manchineel plank. But some of the most considerable articles of their trade are with the Spanish continent of New Spain and Terra Firma; for in the former they cut great quantities of logwood, and both in the former and latter they drive a vast and profitable trade in negroes, and all kinds of the same European goods which are carried thither from Old Spain by the flota.

Both the logwood trade and this counterband have been the subjects of much contention, and the cause of a war between ours and the Spanish nation. The former we avow, and we claim it as our right; though

though in the laſt treaty of peace, that point was far from being well ſettled. The latter we permit; becauſe we think, and very juſtly, that if the Spaniards find themſelves aggrieved by any counterband trade, it lies upon them, and not upon us, to put a ſtop to it.

Formerly we cut logwood in the bay of Campeachy on the northern ſide of the peninſula of Jucatan. But the Spaniards have driven our people entirely from thence, and built forts and made ſettlements to prevent them from returning. Expelled from thence, the logwood cutters ſettled upon the gulph of Honduras on the ſouthern ſide of the ſame peninſula, where they are in ſome ſort eſtabliſhed, and have a fort to protect them. They are an odd kind of people, compoſed moſtly of vagabonds and fugitives from all parts of North America, and their way of life is ſuitable. They live pretty much in a lawleſs manner, though they elect one amongſt them whom they call their king; and to him they pay as much obedience as they think fit. The country they are in is low, and extremely marſhy; the air is prodigiouſly moleſted with muſkettoes; and the water dangerous with alligators; yet a life of licentiouſneſs, a plenty of brandy, large gains, and a want of thought, have perfectly reconciled them to the hardſhips of their employment, and the
unwhol-

unwholfomenefs of the climate. They go always well armed, and are about one thoufand five hundred men.

In the dry feafon, when they cut the logwood, they advance a confiderable way into the country, following the logwood, which runs amongft the other trees of the foreft, like the vein of a mineral in the earth. When the rains have overflowed the whole country, they have marks by which they know where the logwood is depofited. This is an heavy wood, and finks in the water. However, it is eafily buoyed up, and one diver can lift very large beams. Thefe they carry by the favour of the land-floods into the river, to a place which is called the Barcaderas or Port, where they meet the fhips that come upon this trade.

In the year 1716, when the debate concerning this matter was revived; the lords of trade reported, that before the year 1676 we had a number of people fettled and carrying on this trade on the peninfula of Jucatan; that we always confidered this as our right, and were fupported in it by our kings; and that this right was confirmed, if it had wanted any confirmation, by a claufe of *uti poffidetis* in the treaty of peace which was concluded with Spain and the court of London in 1676, and that we certainly were in full poffeffion of thofe fettlements and that trade,

long

long before the time of that treaty; and further, that the Spaniards themfelves have incidentally drawn a great advantage from it, fince the pirates, who were formerly the moft refolved and effectual enemies they ever had, were the more eafily reftrained from their enterprizes, by having their minds diverted to this employment. Upon the whole, they concluded it an affair very well worth the attention of the government, as in fome years it employed near fix thoufand tuns of fhipping; found employment for a number of feamen proportionable; confumed a good deal of our manufactures, and was of confiderable ufe in fabricating many others; and that the whole value of the returns were not lefs than fixty thoufand pounds fterling a year. Notwithftanding this, our claim feems dropped, nor is it very clear how far it can be maintained, to carry on a trade by violence in a country, in which we can hardly claim, according to the common ideas of right in America, any property. However this may be, the trade, though with many difficulties and difcouragements, ftill continues, and will probably continue whilft the Spaniards are fo weak upon that fide of Mexico, and while the coaft continues fo difagreeable, that none but defperate perfons will venture to refide there. The logwood trade is generally carried on by veffels from New England, New York, and Penfyl-

Penſylvania, who take up the goods they want in Jamaica.

But there is a trade yet more profitable carried on between this iſland and the Spaniſh continent, eſpecially in time of war. This too has been the cauſe of much bickering between us and the court of Spain, and it will yet be more difficult for them to put a ſtop to this trade than to the former, whilſt the Spaniards are ſo eager for it, whilſt it is ſo profitable to the Britiſh merchant, and whilſt the Spaniſh officers from the higheſt to the loweſt ſhew ſo great a reſpect to preſents properly made. The trade is carried on in this manner. The ſhip from Jamaica having taken in negroes, and a proper ſortment of goods there, proceeds in time of peace to a harbour called the Grout within Monkey-key, about four miles from Porto-bello. A perſon who underſtands Spaniſh, is directly ſent aſhore to give the merchants of the town notice of the arrival of the veſſel; the ſame news is carried likewiſe with great ſpeed to Panama; from whence the merchants ſet out diſguiſed like peaſants with their ſilver in jars covered with meal, to deceive the officers of the revenue. Here the ſhip remains trading frequently for five or ſix weeks together. The Spaniards uſually come on board, leave their money, and take their negroes, and their goods packed up in parcels fit for one man to carry,

carry, after having been handsomely entertained on board, and receiving provisions sufficient for their journey homeward. If the whole cargo is not disposed of here, they bear off eastward to the Brew, a harbour about five miles distant from Carthagena, where they soon find a vent for the rest. There is no trade more profitable than this; for your payments are made in ready money; and the goods sell higher than they would at any other market. It is not on this coast only, but every where upon the Spanish main, that this trade is carried on; nor is it by the English only, but the French from Hispaniola, the Dutch from Curassou, and even the Danes have some share in it. When the Spanish guarda costas seize upon one of these vessels, they make no scruple of confiscating the cargo, and of treating the crew in a manner little better than pirates.

This commerce in time of peace, and this with the prizes that are made in time of war, pour into Jamaica an astonishing quantity of treasure; great fortunes are made in a manner instantly, whilst the people appear to live in such a state of luxury as in all other places leads to beggary. Their equipages, their cloaths, their furniture, their tables, all bear the tokens of the greatest wealth and profusion imaginable; this obliges all the treasure they receive, to make but a very short stay, as
all

all this treasure added to all the products of the island itself, is hardly more than sufficient to answer the calls of their necessity and luxury on Europe and North America, and their demand for slaves, of which this island is under the necessity of an annual recruit for its own use and that of the Spanish trade, of upwards of six thousand head, and which stand them one with another in thirty pounds apiece, and often more.

CHAP. IV.

Port-Royal. The earthquake 1692. Kingston. St. Jago de la Vega, or Spanish-town. Disputes about the removal of the seat of government.

THE whole island is divided into nineteen districts or parishes, which send each of them two members to the assembly, and allow a competent maintenance to a minister. Port-Royal was anciently the capital of the island; it stood upon the very point of a long narrow neck of land, which towards the sea formed part of the border of a very noble harbour of its own name. In this harbour above a thousand sail of the largest ships could anchor with the greatest convenience and safety; and the water was so deep at the key of Port-Royal, that vessels of the greatest burden

burden could lay their broadsides to the wharfs, and load and unload at little expence or trouble. This conveniency weighed so much with the inhabitants, that they chose in this spot to build their capital, though the place was an hot dry sand, which produced not one of the necessaries of life; no not even fresh water. However, this advantageous situation, and the resort of the pirates, soon made it a very considerable place. It contained two thousand houses very handsomely built, and which rented as high as those in London. It had a resort like a constant fair, by the great concourse of people of business, and grew to all this in about thirty years time; for before that there was scarcely an house upon the place. In short, there were very few places in the world, which for the size could be compared to this town for trade, wealth, and an entire corruption of manners.

It continued thus until the 9th of June 1692, when an earthquake, which shook the whole island to its foundations, overwhelmed this city, and buried nine tenths of it eight fathom under water. This earthquake not only demolished this city, but made a terrible devastation all over the island, and was followed by a contagious distemper, which was near giving the last hand to its ruin. Ever since, it is remarked, that the air is far more unwholsome than formerly.

This

This earthquake, one of the moſt dreadful that I think ever was known, is deſcribed in ſuch lively colours in the Philoſophical tranſactions, and by perſons who ſaw and had a large part in the terrors and loſſes of this calamity, that I ſhall ſay nothing of it, but refer thither; as I am certain no man from his fancy, could aſſemble a greater number of images of horror, than the nature of things, taught the perſons who ſaw them, to bring together, and which are there related very naturally and pathetically.

They rebuilt this city after the earthquake, but it was again deſtroyed. A terrible fire laid it in aſhes about ten years after. Notwithſtanding this, the extraordinary convenience of the harbour tempted them to rebuild it once more. But in the year 1722 a hurricane, one of the moſt terrible on record, reduced it a third time to a heap of rubbiſh. Warned by theſe extraordinary calamities, that ſeemed to mark out this place as a devoted ſpot, by an act of aſſembly they removed the cuſtom-houſe and public offices from thence, and forbid that any market ſhould be held there for the future. The principal inhabitants came to reſide at the oppoſite ſide of the bay, at a place which is called Kingſton. The town is commodiouſly ſituated for freſh water, and all manner of accommodations. The ſtreets are of a commodious wideness, regularly drawn, and cutting each other at equal distances and right angels. It consists of upwards of one thousand houses, many of them handsomely built, though low, with porticoes, and every conveniency for a comfortable habitation in that climate. The harbour was formerly in no good posture of defence, but by the care of the late governor Mr. Knowles, it is now strongly fortified.

The river Cobre, a considerable, but not navigable stream, falls into the sea not far from Kingston. Upon the banks of this river stands St. Jago de la Vega, or Spanish-town; the seat of government, and the place where the courts of justice are held, and consequently the capital of Jamaica, though inferior in size and resort to Kingston. However, this, tho' a town of less business, has more gaity. Here reside many persons of large fortunes, and who make a figure proportionable; the number of coaches kept here is very great; here is a regular assembly; and the residence of the gevernor and the principal officers of the government, who have all very profitable places, conspire with the genius of the inhabitants, ostentatious and expensive, to make it a very splendid and agreeable place. Mr. Knowles, the late governor, made an attempt to remove the seat of government from hence to Kingston, for reasons which, it must be owned, have a very plausible appearance; for it would cer-

tainly

tainly faciliate the carrying on of business, to have the courts of justice and the seat of government as near as possible to the center of commericial affairs. But whether the consideration of a more healthful situation; the division of the advantages of great towns with the several parts of the country, and the mischiefs that might arise from shaking the settled order of things, and prejudicing the property of a great many private people, can weigh against the advantages proposed by this removal, I will not undertake to determine. One thing appears I think very plainly in the contest which this regulation produced; that the opposition was at least as much to the governor as to the measure; and that great natural warmth of temper upon all sides, enflamed and envenomed by a spirit of party which reigns in all our plantations, kindled a flame about this, which, if it had not happened, must have risen to the same height upon some other occasion, since there was a plenty of combustible materials ready upon all sides.

The government of this island is, next to that of Ireland, the best in the king's gift. The standing salary is two thousand five hundred pounds a year. The assembly vote the governor as much more; and this, with the other great profits of his office, make it in the whole little inferior to ten thousand pounds a year.

year. But of the government I shall say little, until I speak of the government of the rest of the plantations, to which this is in all respects alike.

CHAP. V.

Barbadoes. Its savage condition at the first planting. The hardships suffered by the planters. The speedy increase of the island. Its great wealth and number of inhabitants. Its decline. Present state of the island.

THE next island, in point of importance, which we possess in the West-Indies, but the oldest in point of settlement, is Barbadoes. This is one, and by no means the most contemptable one amongst the Windward division of the Caribbee islands. It is not distinctly known when this island was first discovered or settled; but it was probably some time about the year 1625.

When the English first landed here, they found the place the most savage and destitute that can well be imagined. It had not the least appearance of ever having been peopled even by savages. There was no kind of beast of pasture or of prey, no fruit, no herb, nor root fit for supporting the life of man. Yet as the climate was good, and the soil appeared fertile, some gentlemen of small fortunes

fortunes in England refolved to become adventurers thither. But the firft planters had not only the utter defolatenefs of the place, and the extreme want of provifions to ftruggle with, but the trees were fo large, of a wood fo hard and ftubborn, and full of fuch great branches, that they proceeded in the clearing of the ground with a difficulty that muft have worn down any ordinary patience. And even when they had tolerably cleared fome little fpot, the firft produce it yielded for their fubfiftence was fo fmall and ordinary, at the fame time that their fupplies from England were fo flow and precarious, that nothing but the nobleft courage, and a firmnefs which cannot receive too many praifes, could have carried them through the difcouragements which they met in the nobleft work in the world, the cultivating and peopling a deferted part of the globe. But by degrees things were mollified; fome of the trees yielded fuftic for the dyers; cotton and indigo agreed well with the foil; tobacco then becoming fashionable in England anfwered tolerably; and the country began gradually to lay afide its favage difpofition and to fubmit to culture.

Thefe good appearances in America, and the ftorm which fome time after began to gather in England, encouraged many to go over; but ftill the colony received no fort of encouragement

encouragement from the government, which at that time underſtood the advantages of colonies but little; and which was beſides much worſe occupied in ſowing thoſe ſeeds of bitterneſs, which came afterwards ſo terribly to their own lips. The court took no other notice of this iſland than to grant it to a very unworthy and unfaithful favourite, the earl of Carliſle; which, as may be judged, proved of no advantage to the ſettlement.

However, as this colony had the hardieſt breeding, and the moſt laborious infancy of any of our ſettlements, ſo it was far ſtronger in its ſtamina, and grew with greater ſpeed; and that to an height, which if it were not proved beyond any reaſonable doubt, could ſcarcely be believed. For in this ſmall iſland, which is but twenty-five miles in length, and in breadth but fourteen, in little more than twenty years after its firſt ſettlement, that is, in 1650, it contained upwards of fifty thouſand whites of all ſexes and ages, and a much greater number of blacks and Indian ſlaves. The former of which ſlaves they bought; the latter they acquired by means not at all to their honour; for they ſeized upon thoſe unhappy men without any pretence, in the neighbouring iſlands, and carried them into ſlavery. A practice which has rendered the Caribbee Indians irreconcileable to us ever ſince.

This small island, peopled by upwards of one hundred thousand souls, was not yet above half of it cultivated, nor was the industry of the inhabitants at a stand. A little before the period I have mentioned, they learned the method of making sugar; and this enlarging the sphere of their trade, they grew prodigiously rich and numerous.

About this time the government in England, which was then in the hands of Cromwell, confined the trade of Barbadoes to the mother country; before it had been managed altogether by the Dutch. The rigour exercised towards the royal party, obliged several gentlemen of very good families to settle in this island, which was far from being peopled like some other colonies, by fugitives and persons desperate at home. After the restoration it continued still to advance by very hasty strides. Not long after the restoration, king Charles created thirteen baronets from the gentlemen of this island, some of whom were worth ten thousand pounds a year, and none so little as one thousand.

In 1676, which was the meridian of this settlement, their whites were computed to be still much about fifty thousand, but their negroe slaves were increased so as to be upwards of one hundred thousand of all kinds. They employed four hundred sail of ships, one with another of an hundred and fifty tuns, in their trade;

trade; their annual exported produce in sugar, indigo, ginger, cotton, &c. amounted to upwards of three hundred and fifty thousand pounds, and their circulating cash at home was two hundred thousand. It is probable that Holland itself, or perhaps even the best inhabited parts of China were never peopled to the same proportion, nor have they land of the same dimensions, which produces any thing like the same profits. But since that time the island has been much upon the decline. The growth of the French sugar islands, and the settlement of Antegua, St. Christopher's, Nevis, and Montserrat, as well as the greater establishment in Jamaica, have drawn away from time to time a vast number of their people. A terrible contagion, said to be brought over by the troops from England, but more probably derived from the coast of Africa, attacked the island in the year 1692; it raged like a pestilence; twenty have died in a day in their principal town; and all parts of the island suffered in proportion. This sickness continued, with some abatements, for several years, and left an ill disposition in the climate ever afterwards. War raged at the same time with this distemper; and the Barbadians who raised a good number of men, lost many of them in fruitless expeditions against the French islands. The land too began not to yield quite so kindly as it formerly had

had done, and in some places they were obliged to manure it. All these causes contributed to reduce the numbers and opulence of this celebrated island. But it is only in comparison of itself, that it may be considered in any other than the most flourishing condition even at this day; for at this day it contains twenty-five thousand whites, very near eighty thousand negroes, and it ships above twenty-five thousand hogsheads of sugar, to the value of three hundred thousand pounds, besides rum, molasses, cotton, ginger, and aloes; an immense peopling and produce for a country not containing more than one hundred thousand acres of land. By the rise of sugars, the returns of this island are little less than they were in its most flourishing times.

This island can raise near five thousand men of its own militia, and it has generally a regiment of regular troops, though not very compleat. It is fortified by nature all along the windward shore by the rocks and shoals, so as to be near two thirds utterly inaccessible. On the leeward side it has good harbours; but the whole coast is protected by a line of several miles in length, and several forts to defend it at the most material places.

They support their own establishment, which is very considerable, with great credit. The governor's place is worth at least five thousand pounds a year, and the rest of their officers

officers have valuable places. They provide very handfomely for their clergy, who are of the church of England, which is the religion eftablifhed here, as it is in the other iflands. Here are very few diffenters. There is in general an appearance of fomething more of order and decency, and of a fettled people, than in any other colony in the Weft-Indies. They have here a college, founded and well endowed by the virtue and liberality of that great man colonel Chriftopher Codrington, who was a native of this ifland, and who for a great number of amiable and ufeful qualities both in public and private life, for his courage, and his zeal for the good of his country, his humanity, his knowledge and love of literature, was far the richeft production and moft fhining ornament this ifland ever had.

This college does not fo fully anfwer the intentions of the excellent founder, as it might do. If the fund was applied to the education of a number of catechifts for the inftruction of the negroes, fome of them of their own colour, it would be a vaft public advantage, befides the charity, or perhaps the indifpenfible duty of fome fuch work.

This college is in Bridge-town, the capital of this ifland, which before the late fire cóntained about twelve hundred houfes, very handfomely built and inhabited by a numerous and wealthy people. The country of Barbadoes

does has a most beautiful appearance, swelling here and there into gentle hills; shining by the cultivation of every part, by the verdure of the sugar canes, the bloom and fragrance of the number of orange, lemon, lime and citron trees, the guavas, papas, aloes, and a vast multitude of other elegant and useful plants, that rise intermix'd with the houses of the gentlemen which are sown thickly on every part of the island. Even the negroe huts, though mean, contribute to the beauty of the country; for they shade them with plantain trees, which give their villages the appearance of so many beautiful groves. In short, there is no place in the West-Indies comparable to Barbadoes, in point of numbers of people, cultivation of the soil, and those elegancies and conveniencies which result from both.

CHAP. VI.

St. Christopher, Antegua, Nevis, Montserrat; their present condition and force.

THE island of St. Christopher's is the chief of those which we possess amongst the Leeward islands. It was first settled by the French and English in the year 1626, but after various fortunes it was entirely ceded to us by the treaty of Utrecht. This island is about

about seventy-five miles in compass. The circuit of Antegua is but little inferior. Nevis and Montserrat are the smallest of the four, not exceeding for either of them, about eighteen or twenty miles in circumference. The soil in all these islands is pretty much alike; light and sandy, but notwithstanding fertile in an high degree. Antegua has no rivulets of fresh water, and but very few springs; this made it be deemed uninhabitable for a long time; but now they save the rains in ponds and cisterns with great care, and they are rarely in great distress for water. In a word, this island, which we formerly thought useless, has got the start of all the Leeward islands, increasing every day in its produce and inhabitants both freemen and slaves. It has one of the best harbours in the West-Indies; on it stands the principal town called St. John's, which is large and wealthy.

The island of St. Christopher's is not so much on the increase. Neither that, nor any of the Leeward islands, yields any commodity of consequence but what is derived from the cane, except Montserrat, which exports some indigo, but of a very inferior kind.

It is judged that the island of St. Christopher's contains about seven thousand whites, and twenty thousand negroes; that Antegua has also about seven thousand of the former colour, and thirty thousand blacks; and that
Nevis

Nevis and Montferrat may have each about five thousand Europeans, who are the masters of ten or twelve thousand African slaves. So that the whole of the Leeward islands may be reckoned without exaggeration to maintain about twenty thousand English, of whom every single man gives bread to several in England, which is effected by the labour of near seventy thousand negroes. Of the island of Barbuda, I say little, because it has no direct trade with England. It is employed in husbandry, and raising fresh provisions for the use of the neighbouring colonies. It is the property of the Codrington family.

These islands are under the management of one governor, who has the title of captain general and governor in chief of all the Caribbee islands from Guardaloupe to Porto Rico. His post is worth about three thousand five hundred pounds a year. Under him each island has its particular deputy governor at a salary of two hundred pounds a year, and its separate, independent legislative of a council, and an assembly of the representatives.

CHAP.

CHAP. VII.

Climate of the West-Indies. The rains and winds. Hurricanes. Their prognostics. Produce of the West-Indies. Sugar. The manner of manufacturing it. Planters in the West-Indies. Their way of life and management of their affairs. The Negroes.

THE climate in all our West-India islands is nearly the same, allowing for those accidental differences which the several situations, and qualities of the lands themselves produce. As they lie within the tropic, and that the sun goes quite over their heads, passing beyond them to the north, and never retires further from any of them than about 30 degrees to the South, they are continually subjected to the extreme of an heat, which would be intolerable, if the trade wind rising gradually as the sun gathers strength, did not blow in upon them from the sea, and refresh the air in such a manner as to enable them to attend their concerns even under the meridian sun. On the other hand, as the night advances, a breeze begins to be perceived, which blows smartly from the land, as it were from its center, towards the sea, to all points of the compass at once.

By

By the same remarkable providence in the disposing of things it is, that when the sun has made a great progress towards the tropic of Cancer, and becomes in a manner vertical, he draws after him such a vast body of clouds, as shield them from his direct beams, and dissolving into rain cool the air, and refresh the country, thirsty with the long drought, which commonly reigns from the beginning of January to the latter end of May.

The rains in the West-Indies are by no means the things they are with us. Our heaviest rains are but dews comparatively. They are rather floods of water poured from the clouds, with a prodigious impetuosity; the rivers rise in a moment; new rivers and lakes are formed, and in a short time all the low country is under water. Hence it is, that the rivers which have their source within the tropics, swell and overflow their banks at a certain season; and so mistaken were the ancients in their idea of the torrid zone, which they imagined to be dried and scorched up with a continual and fervent heat, and to be for that reason uninhabitable; when in reality some of the largest rivers in the world have their course within its limits, and the moisture is one of the greatest inconveniencies of the climate in several places.

The rains make the only distinction of seasons in the West-Indies; the trees are green the whole year round; they have no cold, no frosts, no snows, and but rarely some hail; the storms of hail are however very violent when they happen, and the hailstones very great and heavy. Whether it be owing to this moisture alone, which alone does not seem to be a sufficient cause, or to a greater quantity of a sulphurous acid, which predominates in the air in this country, metals of all kinds that are subject to the action of such causes, rust and canker in a very short time; and this cause, perhaps, as much as the heat itself, contributes to make the climate of the West-Indies unfriendly and unpleasant to an European constitution.

It is in the rainy season (principally in the month of August, more rarely in July and September,) that they are assaulted by hurricanes; the most terrible calamity to which they are subject from the climate; this destroys at a stroke the labours of many years, and prostrates the most exalted hopes of the planter, and often just at the moment when he thinks himself out of the reach of fortune. It is a sudden and violent storm of wind, rain, thunder and lightening, attended with a furious swelling of the seas, and sometimes with an earthquake; in short, with every circumstance which the elements can assemble, that is terrible and destructive. First, they see, as the prelude to the ensuing havock, whole fields of sugar canes whirled into the air, and scattered over the

the face of the country. The ftrongeft trees of the foreft are torn up by the roots, and driven about like ftubble; their windmills are fwept away in a moment; their works, the fixtures, the ponderous copper boilers, and ftills of feveral hundred weight, are wrenched from the ground, and battered to pieces: their houfes are no protection, the roofs are torn off at one blaft; whilft the rain, which in an hour rifes five feet, rufhes in upon them with an irrefiftible violence.

There are figns, which the Indians of thefe iflands taught our planters, by which they can prognofticate the approach of an hurricane. The hurricane comes on either in the quarters, or at the full change of the moon. If it comes at the full moon, when you are at the change obferve thefe figns. That day you will fee the fky very turbulent; you will obferve the fun more red than at other times; you will perceive a dead calm, and the hills clear of all thofe clouds and mifts which ufually hover about them. In the clefts of the earth, and in the wells, you hear a hollow rumbling found like the rufhing of a great wind. At night the ftars feem much larger than ufual, and furrounded with a fort of burs; the North-weft fky has a black and menacing look; the fea emits a ftrong fmell, and rifes into vaft waves, often without any wind; the wind itfelf now forfakes its ufual fteady Eafterly stream, and shifts about to the West; from whence it sometimes blows with intermissions violently and irregularly for about two hours at a time. You have the same signs at the full of the moon; the moon herself is surrounded with a great bur, and sometimes the sun has the same appearance. These prognostics were taught by the Indians; and in general one may observe, that ignorant country people and barbarous nations, are better observers of times and seasons, and draw better rules from them, than more civilized and reasoning people, for they rely more upon experience than theories, they are more careful of traditionary observations, and living more in the open air at all times, and not so occupied but they have leisure to observe every change, though minute, in that element, they come to have great treasures of useful matter, though, as it might be expected, mixed with many superstitious and idle notions as to the causes. These make their observations to be rejected as chimerical in the gross by many literati, who are not near so nice and circumspect as they ought to be in distinguishing what this sort of people may be very competent judges of, and what not.

The grand staple commodity of the West-Indies is sugar; this commodity was not at all known to the Greeks and Romans, though it was made in China in very early times, from whence

whence we had the first knowledge of it; but the Portuguese were the first who cultivated it in America, and brought it into request as one of the materials of a very universal luxury in Europe. It is not settled whether the cane from which this substance is extracted, be a native of America or brought thither by the Portuguese from India, and the coast of Africa; but however the matter may be, in the beginning they made the most as they still do the best sugars, which come to market in this part of the world. The sugar cane grows to the height of between six and eight feet, full of joints, about four or five inches asunder; the colour of the body of the cane is yellowish, and the top, where it shoots into leaves of a vivid green; the coat is pretty hard, and within contains a spungy substance full of a juice, the most lively, elegant, and least cloying sweet in nature; and which sucked raw, has proved extremely nutritive and wholsome.

They are cultivated in this manner. In the month of August, that is, in the rainy part of the year, after the ground is cleared and well hoed, they lay a piece of six or seven joints of the cane, flat in a channel made for it, above half a foot deep; this they cover with the earth, and so plant the whole field in lines regularly disposed and at proper distances. In a short time a young cane shoots out from every joint of the stock which was interred;

and grows in twelve days to be a pretty tall and vigorous plant; but it is not until after sixteen months, or thereabouts, that the canes are fit to answer the purposes of the planter, though they may remain a few months after without any considerable prejudice to him. The longer they remain in the ground after they are come to maturity, the less juice they afford; but this is somewhat compensated by the superior richness of the juice. That no time may be lost, they generally divide their cane grounds into three parts. One is of standing canes, and to be cut that season; the second is of new planted canes; and the third is fallow, ready to receive a fresh supply. In some places they make second and third cuttings from the same root. The tops of the canes, and the leaves which grow upon the joints, make very good provender for their cattle, and the refuse of the cane after grinding, serves for fire; so that no part of this excellent plant is without its use.

The canes are cut with a billet, and carried in bundles to the mill, which is now generally a windmill; it turns three great cylinders or rollers plated with iron set perpendicularly and cogged so as to be all moved by the middle roller. Between these the canes are bruised to pieces, and the juice runs through an hole into a vat which is placed under the rollers to receive it; from hence it is carried through

through a pipe into a great reservoir, in which however, for fear of turning sour, it is not suffered to rest long; but is conveyed out of that by other pipes into the boiling house, where it is received by a large cauldron: here it remains, until the scum which constantly arises during the boiling, is all taken off; from this, it is passed successively into five or six more boilers, gradually diminishing in their size, and treated in the same manner. In the last of these it becomes of a very thick clammy consistence; but mere boiling is incapable of carrying it farther: to advance the operation, they pour in a small quantity of lime-water; the immediate effect of this alien mixture, is to raise up the liquor in a very vehement fermentation; but to prevent it from running over, a bit of butter no larger than a nut is thrown in, upon which the fury of the fermentation immediately subsides; a vessel of two or three hundred gallons requires no greater force to quiet it. It is now taken out and placed in a cooler, where it dries, granulates, and becomes fit to be put into the pots, which is the last part of the operation.

The pots are conical, or of a sugar-loaf fashion; open at the point, which must be considered as their bottom; here a strainer is put across. In these pots the sugar purges itself of its remaining impurity; the molasses or treacly part disentangles itself from the rest;

precipitates and runs out of the aperture at the bottom; it is now in the conditon called muscavado sugar, of a yellowish brown colour, and thus it is generally put into the hogshead and shipped off.

But when they have a mind to refine it yet further, and leave no remains at all of the molasses, they cover the pots I have just mentioned with a sort of white clay, like that used for tobacco pipes, diluted with water; this penetrates the sugar, unites with the molasses, and with them runs off, leaving the sugar of a whitish colour, but whitest at top. This is called clayed sugar; the operation is sometimes repeated once or twice more, and the sugar every time diminishing in quantity gains considerably in value; but still is called clayed sugar. Further than this they do not go in the plantations, because an heavy duty of sixteen shillings per hundred weight is laid upon all sugars refined there; it is therefore not to my purpose to carry the account any further.

Of the molasses rum is made, in a manner that needs no description, since it differs in nothing from the manner of distilling any other spirit. From the scummings of the sugar, a meaner spirit is procured. Rum finds its market in North America, (where it is consumed by the English inhabitants, or employed in the Indian trade, or distributed from thence to the fishery of Newfoundland, and the African

can commerce;) besides what comes to England and Ireland. However, a very great quantity of molasses is taken off raw and carried to New England to be distilled there.

They compute that when things are well managed, the rum and molasses pay the charges of the plantation, and that the sugars are clear gain. However, by the particulars we have seen, and by others which we may easily imagine, the expences of a plantation in the West-Indies are very great, and the profits at the first view precarious; for the chargeable articles of the windmill, the boiling, cooling and distilling houses, and the buying and subsisting a suitable number of slaves and cattle, will not suffer any man to begin a sugar plantation of any consequence, not to mention the purchase of the land, which is very high, under a capital of at least five thousand pounds. Neither is the life of a planter, a life of idleness and luxury; at all times he must keep a watchful eye upon his overseers, and even oversee himself occasionally. But at the boiling season, if he is properly attentive to his affairs, no way of life can be more laborious, and more dangerous to the health; from a constant attendance day and night in the extreme united heats of the climate and so many fierce furnaces; add to this the losses by hurricanes, earthquakes, and bad seasons; and then consider,

consider, when the sugars are in the cask, that he quits the hazard of a planter, to engage in the hazards of a merchant, and ships his produce at his own risk. The sum of all might make one believe, that it could never answer to engage in this business; but notwithstanding all this, there are no parts of the world, in which great estates are made in so short a time as in the West-Indies. The produce of a few good seasons will provide against the ill effects of the worst; as the planter is sure of a speedy and profitable market for his produce, which has a readier sale than perhaps any other commodity in the world.

Large plantations are generally under the care of a manager or chief overseer, who has commonly a salary of a hundred and fifty pounds a year, with overseers under him in proportion to the greatness of the plantation, one to about thirty negroes, and at the rate of about forty pounds. Such plantations too have a surgeon at a fixed salary employed to take care of the negroes which belong to it. But the course, which is the least troublesome to the owner of the estate, is to let the land with all the works, and the stock of cattle and slaves, to a tenant, who gives security for the payment of the rent, and the keeping up repairs and the stock. The estate is generally estimated to such a tenant at half the neat produce of the

best

best years. Such tenants, if industrious and frugal men, soon make good estates for themselves.

The negroes in the plantations are subsisted at a very easy rate. This is generally by allotting to each family of them a small portion of land, and allowing them two days in the week, Saturday and Sunday, to cultivate it; some are subsisted in this manner, but others find their negroes themselves with a certain portion of Guinea or Indian corn, and to some a salt herring, or a small quantity of bacon or salt pork a day. All the rest of the charge consists in a cap, a shirt, a pair of breeches, stockings and shoes; the whole not exceding forty shillings a year.

To particularise the commodities proper for the West-India market, would be to enumerate all the necessaries, conveniencies, and luxuries of life; for they have nothing of their own but the commodities I have already mentioned. Traders there make a very large profit upon all they sell; and all kind of handicraftsmen, especially carpenters, bricklayers and brasiers, get very great encouragement.

CHAP.

CHAP. VIII.

Observations on the settlement of the West-Indies. Advantages there for tempers prejudicial at home. Bad tempers not always noxious in every sense.

THE disposition to industry has a variety of characters, and is by no means constantly of the same colour. Some acquiesce in a moderate labour through the whole of their lives, attended with no risk either to their persons or their gains; such sort of people, who form the best citizens in general, are fit to stay at home. Others full as remote from an indolent disposition, are of quite a different character. These are fiery, restless tempers, willing to undertake the severest labour, provided it promises but a short continuance, who love risk and hazard, whose schemes are always vast, and who put no medium between being great and being undone. Characters of this sort, especially when they happen in low and middling life, are often dangerous members in a regular and settled community. But the West-Indies opens a fair and ample field to encourage persons of such a disposition; and it may be reckoned one very great benefit of our possessions in that part of the world, that besides the vast quantities

tities of our fabrics which they confume, our feamen that they employ, and our revenues that they fupport, that they are a vent to carry off fuch fpirits, whom they keep occupied greatly to the public benefit. Our dominions are fo circumftanced, and afford fuch a variety, that all difpofitions to bufinefs, of what kind foever, may have exercife without preffing upon one another. It is befides a great happinefs, that unfortunate men, whom unavoidable accidents, the frowns of the world, or the cruelty of creditors, would have rendered miferable to themfelves, and ufelefs to the public, may find a fort of afylum, where at laft they often fucceed fo well, as to have reafon to blefs thofe accidents, which drove them from their country poor, deferted and defpifed, to return them to it in opulence and credit. Of fuch a change every one can produce many inftances of his own knowledge; as whoever looks about him cannot fail to fee a great number of perfons, who having taken wrong fteps in the beginning of their lives, have eftablifhed fuch a character of weaknefs and imprudence, as prevents them ever after from being trufted or employed, wherever they are at all known, although their characters fhould be altogether changed and the paffions quite fubfided which gave occafion to their errors. Such perfons become, firft, indigent, then defperate, and at laft, abandoned;

ed; but when they have an opportunity of going where this prejudice does not operate againſt them, they ſet up as new men. With the advantage of an experience acquired by their miſtakes, they are free from the ill reputation which attended them; and they prove of vaſt ſervice to their country, to which they could be of no advantage whilſt they remained in it. There are perſons too, far more blameable than either of the former ſorts, who having erred without proper caution in points of morality, are deſervedly regarded with diſtruſt and abhorrence, though they may be at bottom far from being utterly abandoned; and are ſtill, excepting their character, the ſtuff proper for making very good men of the world.

Theſe are the ſeveral ſorts of people, who with very few exceptions, have ſettled the Weſt-Indies, and North America in a good meaſure. And thus have we drawn from the raſhneſs of hot and viſionary men; the imprudence of youth; the corruption of bad morals; and even from the wretchedneſs and miſery of perſons deſtitute and undone, the great ſource of our wealth, our ſtrength and our power. And though this was neither the effect of our wiſdom, nor the conſequence of our foreſight; yet having happened, it may tend to give us more wiſdom and a better foreſight; for it will undoubtedly be a ſtanding

ing monitor to us, how much we ought to cherish the colonies we have already established, by every encouragement in our power, and by every reasonable indulgence; and it will be an additional spur to make us active in the acquisition of new ones. Since experience has taught us, that as there is no soil or climate which will not shew itself grateful to culture, so that there is no disposition, no character in mankind, which may not be turned with dextrous management to the public advantage. Those rulers, who make complaints of the temper of their people in almost any respect, ought rather to lament their own want of genius, which blinds them to the use of an instrument purposely put into their hands by Providence, for effecting perhaps the greatest things. There are humours in the body, which contained may be noxious to it, yet which sent abroad are the proper materials for generating new bodies. Providence, and a great minister who should imitate Providence, often gain their ends by means that seem most contrary to them; for earthquakes, and hurricanes, and floods, are as necessary to the well-being of things, as calm and sun-shine; life and beauty are drawn from death and corruption; and the most efficacious medicines are often found united with the most deadly poisons. This, as it is well known, is the order of nature, and perhaps it it might not unwisely be considered, as an example for government.

CHAP. IX.

Observations on taxing the colonies. On an expensive establishment there. Objections answered.

THOUGH we have drawn such great advantages from our possessions in the West-Indies, and are, even in our present way of acting, likely to continue to draw still more; and though we have not wholly neglected the culture of that useful province; yet some will think, there are some things yet left undone, some things in which our neighbours have set us a laudable example, and some others which the inconveniencies we have felt from the want of them demonstrate to be necessary to ourselves. But it is not my purpose to handle this subject in its full extent, since it is the wisdom and power of the legislature, and not the unauthorized speculations of a private man, which can effect any thing useful in this way. A West-Indian who is naturally warm in his temper, and not too servilely obedient to the rules of the bienseance, might find some faults in our proceedings here, and would perhaps reason in a manner not unlike the following.

" One

"One would think from some instances, that at the distance we are placed from the seat of authority, we were too remote to enjoy its protection, but not to feel its weight. Innumerable are the grievances which have oppressed us from our infancy, and which contribute to bring on us a premature old age. Not one of the least evils under which our plantations in the West-Indies groan, is the support of an expensive civil establishment, suited rather to an established and independent country in the plenitude of wealth and power, than to newly settled colonies, to which nobody thinks himself to belong as to his country, and which struggle with a total want of almost all the necessaries and conveniencies of life. The building and maintaining the public works and fortifications, is a weight to which we are totally unequal, and the laying of which upon our shoulders is directly contrary to the very purpose for which you cultivate the colonies; for though the produce of these colonies is in general to be considered as a luxury, yet is it of the greatest value to you; first, as it supplies you with things, which if not from us, you must certainly take from foreign nations. Even in this view the colonies are extremely useful. But there is another, and a much more advantageous light in which you may view them; you may consider them as they supply you with a commodity which you export to other

other countries, and which helps to bring the balance of trade in your favour.

The whole secret of managing a foreign market, is contained in two words, to have the commodity of a good kind, and to sell it cheap; and the whole domestic policy of trade consists in contriving to answer these two ends, and principally the latter. Now, by what magic can we effect to sell as cheap as the French at any foreign market, when our planters pay four and a half per cent. duty upon all the sugars, which they ship off in America, and this after having had the same commodity in effect heavily taxed before by the poll on the negroes which work it, and by other impositions, which the planters endure according to the exigencies of the government? when the French planter pays a very insignificant poll-tax at worst, and not one per cent. duty upon all the sugars he exports; when he buys his negroes at an easier rate than we can do; when he is more favoured upon every occasion, and is besides of a temper more industrious and frugal, than is found in our people. Besides this, upon sudden emergencies we run very much in debt; the island of Barbadoes at one stroke expended thirty thousand pounds upon a fortification, to say nothing of what this and what other islands have done in the same way and upon similar occasions? We are in reality only your factors; you in England ought to consider yourselves

as

as the merchants, who should be at the whole expence, and should willingly abide by whatsoever loss accrues; since the profits are all your own, and since in the end by the course of trade, the loss too, let you take what shifting measures you please to avoid it, and to cheat yourselves with appearances. It is reasonable that you should lay what duty you please upon what is consumed amongst yourselves, because you govern that market as you please; but what you charge, or suffer to be charged on the islands, is only the price of your own goods enhanced so much at the foreign market; there you have no exclusive privilege, and there you are sure to suffer. If that duty which is laid in England upon the produce of our islands, or even half of it were expended, as in reason it ought, for the support of our establishment, we might well be freed from the heavy burdens which we bear, and consequently might be somewhat upon a par with our neighbours. In our present condition, we not only pay very ample salaries to our governors, but they are besides suffered to make the most they can by management of our weakness, to cheat us into voluntary gratuities, which we have given often without a due consideration of our circumstances. This custom prompts our governors to use a thousand arts equally unbecoming their character, and prejudicial to the provinces they govern. It is this which induces them to foment those divisions which tear us to pieces; and which prevent us from attending seriously and entirely to what will best advance the prosperity of our settlements.

It were a tedious and disagreeable task, to run through all the mischiefs of which that one error of sending a governor to make the most he can of us is the fruitful source. The governor, I allow, ought to have every where a certain, reasonable, and even a genteel salary; but then, when he has this, he ought not to be in a condition to hope for any thing further, and ought to consider nothing but how he may best perform the duty of his office.

But I hear it objected, that we are already extremely chargeable to England, who sends her troops to protect us, and her fleets to cover our trade, at a very great expence, for which we ought to be contented, and even thankful; and that it is unreasonable to expect she should bear every part of our burden, loaded as she is with the weight of a vast national debt, and a most expensive establishment of her own. But to this my answer is short, plain, and practical. The French do all this. They send armies and fleets to protect their colonies as well as you; but they support the establishment in their own plantations notwithstanding; and they are far from supposing

posing this an insupportable burden. They know that a little judicious expence is often the best œconomy in the world, and that in this case, it is only sparing their own subjects in the West-Indies, and levying the money laid out for their use upon the foreign consumer. What they do, I see no impossibility of our doing. They learned many of their maxims of trade, as well as many of the fabrics which supply it, from us; I wish we would learn from them in our turn. We have, indeed, some years ago eased the trade, by permitting ships from the islands to carry our produce out directly to foreign markets; but still it is so clogged, that we do not feel all the benefit which we might expect from a more general and better regulated liberty.

Not to carry our enquiries further, see what you have gained by prohibiting us to land our sugars directly in Ireland, before they are first entered in an English port. What was the consequence? why your sugars grew dear by this loading and unloading, and passing backward and forward. The Portuguese offered sugars of at least equal goodness, and at a much more moderate price. The merchants in Ireland would not refuse so good an offer out of a compliment to you, who in this instance paid them no compliment at all; and you cannot, for very good reasons, dispute with the Portuguese about it. If this has happened at home, the confequence muft be infinitely worfe abroad. But it is faid that our failures abroad are only owing to this; that we have not ground enough conveniently fituated to produce more fugars than fatisfies the home demand. But this is far enough from the cafe. There is in feveral of the iflands, but there is in Jamaica in particular, a great quantity of good land, and well enough fituated too, if means were taken to bring it into culture, and a choice of markets to animate the planter in the cultivation; who certainly deferves every fort of encouragement, as he afks for nothing but to be put into fuch a condition, as may enable him to be of more fervice to his mother country."

CHAP. X.

State of the negroes in the Weft-Indies. Danger from them. Methods propofed for remedying thefe abufes. The neceffity of increafing the whites. Ufe of this rgulation in trade.

IN the foregoing manner the Weft-Indian would ftate fome part of what he conceives to be his grievances, and thofe I believe he would be earneft enough to have remedied. But there are other regulations, which a perfon not concerned in their affairs might think very proper too, but which the

Weft-

West-Indian would enter into with a much greater degree of phlegm.

There are now allowed to be in our West-Indies at least two hundred and thirty thousand negro slaves; and it is allowed too that upon the highest calculation the whites there, in all, do not amount to ninety thousand souls. This disproportion shews so clearly at the first glance how much the colonies are endangered, both from within and without; how much exposed to the assaults of a foreign enemy, and to the insurrection of their own slaves, (which latter circumstance in all our islands keeps the people in perpetual apprehensions) that it may be a just cause of surprize, that no measures whatsoever are taken to correct this dangerous irregularity.

This disproportion between the freemen and negroes grows more visible every day. That enterprising spirit which the novelty of the object and various concurrent causes had produced in the last century, has decayed very much. We have as many men indigent and unemployed at home as we had then; but they have not the same spirit and activity they had at that time. The disposition of the people in the West-Indies concurs with that of our people at home, to increase and to perpetuate the evil of which I complain; for they chuse to do every thing by negroes, which can possibly be done by them; and though they have laws

laws and ordinances to oblige them to keep a certain number of white servants in some proportion to their blacks, in most places these laws are but a dead letter. They find it more easy to pay the penalty when seldom it is exacted, than to comply with the law. Their avarice in the particulars makes them blind to the hazards to which they expose the sum total of their affairs. This disposition in the planters is now almost grown inveterate, and to such a degree, that the remedy will probably never be administered by themselves; and if this disposition continues, in a little time, (which is indeed nearly the case already,) all the English in our colonies there will consist of little more than a few planters and merchants; and the rest will be a despicable, though a dangerous, because a numerous and disaffected herd of African slaves.

Indubitably the security, as well as the solid wealth of every nation, consists principally in the number of low and middling men of a free condition, and that beautiful gradation from the highest to the lowest, where the transitions all the way are almost imperceptible. To produce this ought to be the aim and mark of every well regulated commonwealth, and none has ever flourished upon other principles. But when we consider the colony out of that independent light, and as it is related to Great Britain, it is clear that this neglect

neglect is of great detriment to the mother country; becaufe it is certain, that the confumption of our commodities there would be in a great meafure in proportion to the number of white men; and there is nobody at all acquainted with the plantations, who will not readily allow, that when I fay one white man takes off as much of our manufactures as three negroes, that I eftimate his value to us at a very low rate.

But the neceffity of having there a proper number of whites is not only ftrongly enforced by the confideration of the great gain which would from thence accrue to us, but from the vaft favings which fuch an arrangement would produce. The militia of the Weft-Indies is exceedingly well trained, fo as to be in difcipline not very much inferior, but in courage and fpirit beyond moft regular troops; and they really want nothing but fufficient numbers to be able fully to defend themfelves, and occafionally to annoy the enemy; for both which purpofes they are infinitely more fit by being habituated to the climate, than raw troops, which in this part of the world can never meet the enemy in the field with much more than half their complement. A lefs number of troops would do there in all times, if this point was well ftudied; and I may venture to fay, that the tranfporting and comfortably providing for a proper number of men effectually to fecure our colonies, and even to make any attempt upon them desperate, would not have cost the government one third part of the money, which for these twenty years past has been expended in the transporting and maintaining of troops there, who die and waste away without any benefit to themselves or their country; whereas these settlers, who would so effectually intimidate a foreign enemy, and take away all hope of liberty from the negroes, would all the while be enriching their mother country, and paying a large interest for the sums she expended in their establishment.

I am conscious that many objections will be made against the very proposal, and that many more would be started against any effectual scheme for increasing the number of white servants in the West-Indies. They are represented, as of very little use, disorderly, idle, drunken, and fitter to pervert the negroes, than to be any assistance to them in their business. This I believe to be in general true; but this is no sort of objection to having them; though it is an excellent argument for putting them, their masters, and the whole colony under a better regulation. If we labour under great inconveniencies from the want of a police at home, this want is infinitely more visible in the West-Indies, where for the most part they all live without the least sense of religion, in a state of vice and debauchery, which is

really

really deplorable to confider them as men and chriftians, and of a very bad afpect in a political light. If therefore it fhould be thought convenient by the wifdom of our government, at any time to enter into a fcheme for peopling thefe countries fully and properly, it will be equally convenient at the fame time to take fuch ftrict meafures as may preferve them from vice and idlenefs; a thing far enough from impracticable. Whenever fuch regulations fhall take place, they will in a good meafure anfwer another end too, the preferving the health and lives of the people; a point which in all places every wife government will have very much at heart; but which is above all neceffary in a colony, where the people are an ineftimable treafure, and where the climate itfelf is fufficiently fatal.

Thefe obfervations principally regard Jamaica, the largeft and beft of our iflands, where there are prodigious tracts of uncultivated land. As the rivers there are not navigable, and as fugar is a bulky commodity which cannot afford to pay for a very long land carriage, the coafts, or only the land very near the coafts, can be turned to that commodity. But if poor people were fufficiently encouraged to fettle in the inland parts, neceffity would oblige them to raife cotton, cacao, coffee, ginger, aloes, allfpice, the dying woods, and other things which require no vaft vast labour, are not so burdensome in carriage, and which have all a sufficient demand at home to encourage people who do not look to great and sudden fortunes. And as we bring all these, especially the cotton, which is of great use in our manufactures, from abroad, we might encourage the raising more of it by some moderate premium. The same necessity too would oblige them to try experiments on cochineal, and various other things which we don't now think of, and which the climate would not refuse. By degrees, and with good management, they would improve in the culture of many of these articles in which they are now defective; the careful would grow tolerably rich; and considerable works of many valuable commodities, as cacao, cochineal, and even indigo, may be attempted with small capitals. Excepting the labour, I don't know that any of these require above two or three hundred pounds to begin with. So that whilst the great stocks, and the lands convenient to navigation are employed in sugars, the small capitals and the inland might be employed in the less expensive, though not less useful articles I have mentioned; every part would flourish, and agriculture would have its share with the other improvements; so that the great number might be subsisted at less expence than the few are now maintained. All this,

this, I am confident, could be effected for twenty thousand pounds, or less, properly laid out; and the island by this means be rendered in a few years three times more beneficial to us than it is at present. By the neglect of some encouragement of this kind, the great stocks, and the running into a staple which required them, have by degrees devoured the island. It is the nature of vast stocks to create a sort of monopoly; and it is the nature of monopoly to aim at great profits from a comparatively little produce; but diffuse business, and by bringing it within the compass of several, you will make them sit down each with a small profit, for all cannot hope a fortune, but the joint produce of all will be very considerable. Indigo was once very greatly produced in Jamaica, and it enriched the island to so great a degree, that in the parish of Vere, where this drug was cultivated, they are said to have had no less than three hundred gentlemen's coaches; a number I do not imagine even the whole island exceeds at this day; and there is great reason to believe, that there were many more persons of property in Jamaica formerly than are there now, though perhaps they had not those vast fortunes, which dazzle us in such a manner at present.

CHAP.

CHAP. XI.

Misery of the negroes. Great waste of them. Methods of preventing it. Instruction of negroes in religion.

SINCE I have indulged myself so long in a speculation, which appears to me very material to the welfare of these colonies, I shall venture to say something farther concerning another part of the inhabitants, tho' it may perhaps meet no warm reception from those who are the most nearly concerned.

The negroes in our colonies endure a slavery more compleat, and attended with far worse circumstances, than what any people in their condition suffer in any other part of the world, or have suffered in any other period of time. Proofs of this are not wanting. The prodigious waste which we experience in this unhappy part of our species, is a full and melancholy evidence of this truth. The island of Barbadoes, (the negroes upon which do not amount to eighty thousand) notwithstanding all the means which they use to increase them by propagation, notwithstanding that the climate is in every respect, except that of being more wholesome, exactly resembling the climate from whence they come; notwithstanding all this, Barbadoes lies under a neceffity of an annual recruit of five thoufand flaves to keep up the ftock at the number I have mentioned. This prodigious failure, which is at leaft in the fame proportion in all our iflands, fhews demonftratively that fome uncommon and infupportable hardfhip lies upon the negroes which wears them down in fuch a furprifing manner; and this, I imagine, is principally the exceffive labour which they undergo. For previoufly, I fuppofe, that none of the inhabitants of the countries between the tropics are capable, even in their own climates, of near fo much labour without great prejudice to them, as our people are in ours. But in our plantations the blacks work feverely for five days, without any relaxation or intermiffion, for the benefit of the mafter; and the other two days they are obliged to labour for their own fubfiftence during the reft of the week; and this, I imagine, with the other circumftances of great feverity which deprefs their fpirits, naturally cuts off great numbers, as well as difqualifies thofe who remain from fupplying this wafte by natural propagation.

The planter will fay, that if he is to allow his negroes more recreation, and to indulge them in more hours of abfence from their work, he can never reimburfe himfelf for the charge he has been at in the purchafe of the flave, nor make the profits which induced him

him to go to that expence. But this, though it appears plausible enough at first, because the slaves are very dear, and because they do not yield above ten or twelve pounds a head annually clear profit by their labour, is notwithstanding very fallacious. For let it be considered, that out of their stock of eighty thousand in Barbadoes, there die every year five thousand negroes more than are born in that island: in effect this people is under a necessity of being entirely renewed every sixteen years; and what must we think of the management of a people, who far from increasing greatly, as those who have no loss by wars ought to do, must in so short a space of time as sixteen years, without foreign recruits, be entirely consumed to a man? Let us suppose that these slaves stand the Barbadians in no more than twenty pounds a head out of the ship; whereas, in reality, they cost a great deal more; this makes one hundred thousand pounds every year, and in sixteen years one million six hundred thousand pounds. A sum really astonishing, and amounting to a fourth of the value of every thing they export.

Now suppose, that by allowing a more moderate labour, and some other indulgences, a great number of these deaths might be prevented, (and many I think it is probable would so be prevented,) and that they could keep up within a thousand of their stock, (and why they

they could entirely keep it up by such means, I cannot possibly guess) they would save in this way eighty thousand pounds every year. But from thence we must deduct the time in which these slaves have been unemployed. I suppose that all reasonable indulgences might be given of every sort for the difference of forty thousand pounds, which is the labour of four thousand slaves. This will be far from a small allowance, especially as in this way less time will be lost by sickness, and the surgeon will have less employment. Then, after all deductions, by behaving like good men, good masters, and good christians, the inhabitants of this one island would save forty thousand pounds a year; which if instead of being saved, it were lost by such a proceeding, it ought to be considered as a necessary loss, and borne accordingly.

This matter, though not I think before shewn in this same light, seems in itself extremely clear; but if it were yet clearer, there are several gentlemen of the West-Indies who could not comprehend it; though a waggoner in England will comprehend very clearly, that if he works his horse but moderately, and feeds him well, he will draw more profit from him in the end, than if he never gave him an hour's respite in the day from his work, and at night turned him upon the common for his subsistence. I am far from contending

tending in favour of an effeminate indulgence to these people. I know that they are stubborn and intractable for the most part, and that they must be ruled with a rod of iron. I would have them ruled, but not crushed with it. I would have a humanity exercised which is consistent with steadiness. And I think it clear from the whole course of history, that those nations which have behaved with the greatest humanity to their slaves, were always best served, and ran the least hazard from their rebellions. And I am the more convinced of the necessity of these indulgences, as slaves certainly cannot go through so much work as freemen. The mind goes a great way in every thing; and when a man knows that his labour is for himself; and that the more he labours, the more he is to acquire, this consciousness carries him through, and supports him beneath fatigues, under which he otherwise would have sunk.

The prejudice this saving would be to the African trade, is I know an objection which to some would appear very plausible. But surely, one cannot hear without horror of a trade which must depend for its support upon the annual murder of several thousands of innocent men; and indeed nothing could excuse the slave trade at all, but the necessity we are under of peopling our colonies, and the consideration that the slaves we buy were in the same

same condition in Africa, either hereditary, or taken in war. But in fact, if the waste of these men should become less, the price would fall; then if a due order were taken the same demand might be kept, by the extending our colonies, which is now produced by the havock made of the people. This is the case on the continent, where though the slaves increase, there is an annual call for seven thousand at least.

The principal time I would have reserved for the indulgence I propose to be granted to the slaves, is Sunday, or the Lord's day; a day which is profaned in a manner altogether scandalous in our colonies. On this day, I would have them regularly attend at church; I would have them, particularly the children, carefully (full as carefully as any others) instructed in the principles of religion and virtue, and especially in the humility, submission and honesty which become their condition. The rest of the day might be devoted to innocent recreation; to these days of relaxation, and with the same exercises, should be added some days in the grand festival of Christmass, Easter and Whitsuntide, and perhaps, four or five days in the year besides. Such methods would by degrees habituate their masters, not to think them a sort of beasts, and without souls, as some of them do at present, who treat them accordingly; and the slaves would of course grow more honeſt, tractable, and leſs of eye-ſervants; unleſs the ſanctions of religion, the precepts of morality, and all the habits of an early inſtitution, be of no advantage to mankind. Indeed I have before me an * author, if he may be ſo called, who treats the notion of bringing the negroes to chriſtianity with contempt, and talks of it at the beſt, as a thing of indifference. But beſides that he appears to me a writer of very little judgment, I cannot conceive with what face any body, who pretends to inform the public, can ſet up as an advocate for irreligion, barbariſm, and groſs ignorance.

CHAP. XII.

Propoſal for a ſort of enfranchiſement of mulattoes and negroes. Danger from the multitude of houſe negroes.

IT is ſaid, that the law of England is favourable to liberty; and ſo far this obſervation is juſt, that when we had men in a ſervile condition amongſt us, the law took advantage even of neglects of the maſters to enfranchiſe the villain; and ſeemed for that purpoſe even to ſubtilize a little; becauſe our anceſtors judged, that freemen were the real ſupport of the kingdom. What if in our colonies we ſhould

---

* Oldmixon.

should go so far, as to find out some medium between liberty and absolute slavery, in which we might place all mulattoes after a certain limited servitude to the owner of the mother; and such blacks, who being born in the islands, their masters for their good services should think proper in some degree to enfranchise? These might have land allotted them, or where that could not be spared, some sort of fixed employment, from either of which they should be obliged to pay a certain moderate rent to the public. Whatever they should acquire above this, to be the reward of their industry. The necessity of paying the rent would keep them from idleness; and when men are once set to work through necessity, they will not stop there; but they will gradually strive for conveniencies, and some even for superfluities. All this will add to the demand for our goods, and the colony will be strengthened by the addition of so many men, who will have an interest of their own to fight for.

There is, amongst others, a very bad custom in our colonies of multiplying their houshold slaves far beyond reason and necessity. It is not uncommon for families of no very great fortunes, to have twenty-five or thirty in the capacity of menial servants only. These are so many hands taken from planting, to be of no manner of use to the public; but they are infinitely

infinitely the most dangerous of the slaves; for being at all times about our people, they come to abate of that great reverence, which the field negroes have for the whites, without losing any thing of the resentment of their condition, which is common to both. And besides, in any insurrection they have it more in their power to strike a sudden and fatal blow. Surely a sumptuary law might be contrived to restrain the number of the menial slaves, as there might and ought to be one strictly enjoining all who keep five servants, to have one white man and one white woman amongst them, without any power of being indulged in a contrary practice; as it ought to be a rule never to be broken through, to have not only the overseers, but even all the drivers, white men.

The alarms we are under at the news of any petty armament in the West-Indies, is a demonstrative proof of the weakness of our condition there; which is, however, so far from rousing us to seek any proper remedy, that there are not wanting of the people of that country, many who would use a thousand pretences to prevent our taking the only possible means of securing their own possessions from danger; as the majority of men will always be found ready to prefer some present gain to their future and more permanent interests. But the apparent and
dangerous

dangerous progress of the French ought, methinks, to rouse us from our long inaction, and to animate us to enterprise some regulations, in a strain of policy far superior to any thing I have ventured to hint, for the interest of the commerce, and the honour of the councils of the British nation.

PART VII.

British North America.

CHAP. I.

A general view of the English dominions in North America.

IT is somewhat difficult to ascertain the bounds of the English property in North America, to the Northern and Western sides; for to the Northward, it should seem, that we might extend our claims quite to the pole itself, nor does any nation seem inclined to dispute the property of this Northernmost country with us. France has by the treaty of Utrecht, ceded to us Hudson's bay, the streights of Hudson, and all the country bordering upon that bay and those streights. If we should chuse to take our stand upon the Northern extremity of New Britain, or Terra de Labrador, and look towards the South, we have a territory extending in that aspect from the 60th to the 31st degree of North latitude, and consequently more than seventeen hundred miles long in a direct line. This country is, all the way, washed by the Atlantic ocean on the East; to the South it has the small remains of the Spanish Florida; but to the Westward, our bounds are disputed by our enemies, and do not seem well agreed upon amongst ourselves. They who govern themselves by the charters to our colonies, run their jurisdiction quite across the continent to the South-Sea; others contract our rights to the hither banks of the Missisippi, and take four of the great lakes into our dominions, But upon what grounds they have fixed upon that river as a barrier, other than that rivers or mountains seem to be a species of natural boundaries, I cannot determine. Others (upon the same grounds, I suppose,) have contracted us within limits yet narrower; they make the Apalachian mountains, the lake Ontario, and the river St. Laurence, the most Westerly frontier of our rights in America. The French agreeing, in some respects, with these latter, (or the latter rather agreeing with the French, whose maps they have for a long time servilely and shamefully copied,) have made the mountains hem us in from their Southern commencement, to about the 44th degree

degree of North latitude, or thereabouts, where this long chain terminates; then they draw a line flanting to the North-East, by which they cut off a great part of the provinces of New York, New England, and Nova Scotia, and leave our bounds at such a distance from the river St. Laurence, as they judge convenient.

This distribution, and the military dispositions which the French have made to support it, form the principal cause of the quarrel which now subsists between the two kingdoms; and it is the issue of this quarrel, which must instruct future geographers in adjusting the boundaries of the two nations. For the present, I shall only mention what we have settled, without offering any opinion of my own concerning our bounds. Our rights in Nova Scotia have been already ascertained and established in a clear and cogent manner; but with regard to our claims in the Ohio and Missisippi, the rashness of some writers in a matter which is a public concern, seems to me very blameable. Some of them timidly or ignorantly drawing our territories into a very inconvenient narrowness; whilst others have madly claimed all North America from sea to sea; some would give us very narrow bounds, whilst others will hear of no bounds at all.

Posterity

Posterity will perhaps think it unaccountable, that in a matter of such importance we could have been so thoughtless as to leave on our back such a nation as France, without determining, in any manner, even sufficiently clear to settle our own demands, what part of the country was our own right, or what we determined to leave to the discretion of our neighbours; or that wholly intent upon settling the sea coast, we have never cast an eye into the country, to discover the necessity of making a barrier against them, with a proper force; which formerly did not need to have been a very great one, nor to be maintained at any great expence. That cheap and timely caution would have saved us thousands of lives and millions of money; but the hour is now passed.

In the ensuing discourse, I think it better neither to consider our settlements directly in the order of the time of their establishment, nor of their advantage to the mother country, but as they lie near one another, North and South from New England to Carolina; reserving for the end the new settlements on the Northern and Southern extremities, those of Nova Scotia and Georgia, and the unsettled countries about Hudson's bay.

CHAP.

CHAP. II.

First attempts to settle North America. The rise and progress of the puritans. They are persecuted by Laud. Several fly into New England.

WE derive our rights in America from the discovery of Sebastian Cabot, who first made the Northern continent in 1497. The fact is sufficiently certain to establish a right to our settlements in North America: but the particulars are not known distinctly enough to encourage me to enter into a detail of his voyage. The country was in general called Newfoundland, a name which is now appropriated solely to an island upon its coast. It was a long time before we made any attempt to settle this country; though in this point we were no more backward than our neighbours, who probably did not abstain so long out of respect to our prior discovery. Sir Walter Raleigh shewed the way, by planting a colony in the Southern part, which he called Virginia. However, the spirit of colonization was not yet fully raised. Men lived at ease in their own country, and the new settlement of Virginia, though dressed up in all the showy colours which eloquence could bestow upon it, gave adventurers but little encou-

encouragement. The affairs of North America were in the hands of an exclusive company, and they prospered accordingly.

Things remained in this condition until the latter end of the reign of James the first. From the commencement of the reformation in England, two parties of protestants subsisted amongst us; the first had chosen gradually and almost imperceptibly to recede from the church of Rome; softening the lines, rather than erasing the figure, they made but very little alteration in the appearances of things. And the people seeing the exterior so little altered, hardly perceived the great changes they had made in the doctrines of their religion. The other party of a warmer temper, had more zeal and less policy. Several of them had fled from the persecution in queen Mary's days; and they returned in those of queen Elizabeth with minds sufficiently heated by resentment of their sufferings; and by the perpetual disputations which had exercised them all the while they were abroad. Abroad they learned an aversion to the episcopal order, and to religious ceremonies of every sort; they were impregnated with an high spirit of liberty, and had a strong tendency to the republican form of government. Queen Elizabeth had enough of the blood of Harry the eighth, to make her impatient of an opposition to her will, especially in matters of religion,

gion, in which she had an high opinion of her own knowledge. She advised with the party but very little in the alterations which she thought proper to make; and disliking the notions, which they seemed to entertain in politics, she kept them down during the whole course of her reign with an uniform and inflexible severity.

However, the party was far enough from being destroyed. The merit of their sufferings, the affected plainness of their dress, the gravity of their deportment, the use of scripture phrases upon the most ordinary occasions, and even their names, which had something striking and venerable, as being borrowed from the old testament, or having a sort of affected relation to religious matters, gained them a general esteem amongst sober people of ordinary understandings. This party was very numerous; and their zeal made them yet more considerable than their numbers. They were commonly called puritans.

When king James came to the throne, he had a very fair opportunity of pacifying matters; or at worst he might have left them in the condition he found them; but it happened quite otherwise. The unkingly disputation at Hampton-court did more to encourage the puritans to persevere in their opinions, by the notice which was taken of them, than all king James's logic, as a scholar, backed with
all

all his power as a king, could do to suppress that party. They were persecuted, but not destroyed; they were exasperated, and yet left powerful; and a severity was exercised towards them, which at once exposed the weakness and the ill intentions of the government.

In this state things continued until the accession of Charles, when they were far from mending. This prince, endowed with many great virtues, had very few amiable qualities. As grave as the puritans themselves, he could never engage the licentious part of the world in his favour; and that gravity being turned against the puritans, made him but the more odious to them. He gave himself up entirely to the church and churchmen; and he finished his ill conduct in this respect, by conferring the first ecclesiastical dignity of the kingdom, and a great sway in temporal affairs, upon doctor Laud. Hardly fit to direct a college, he was called to govern a kingdom. He was one of those indiscreet men of good intentions, who are the people in the world that make the worst figure in politics. This man thought he did good service to religion by a scrupulous enquiry into the manner in which the ministers every where conformed to the regulations of the former reigns. He deprived great numbers for nonconformity. Not satisfied with this, in which perhaps he was justifiable enough,

enough, if he had managed prudently, he made new regulations, and introduced on a people already abhorrent of the moſt neceſſary ceremonies, ceremonies of a new kind, of a moſt uſeleſs nature, and ſuch as were even ridiculous, if the ſerious conſequences which attended them may not intitle them to be confidered as matters of importance.

Several great men, difguſted at the proceedings of the court, and entertaining very reaſonable apprehenſions for the public liberty, to make themſelves popular, attached themſelves to the popular notions of religion, and affected to maintain them with great zeal. Others became puritans through principle. And now their affairs put on a reſpectable appearance; in proportion as they became of conſequence, their ſufferings ſeemed to be more and more grievous; the ſeverities of Laud raiſed not terror as formerly, but a ſort of indignant hatred; and they became every day further and further from liſtening to the leaſt terms of agreement with ſurplices, organs, common-prayer, or table at the Eaſt-end of the church. As they who are ſerious about trifles, are ſerious indeed, their lives began to grow miſerable to ſeveral on account of theſe ceremonies; and rather than be obliged to ſubmit to them, there was no part of the world to which they would not have fled with chearfulneſs.

Early

Early in the reign of king James a number of perfons of this perfuafion had fought refuge in Holland; in which, though a country of the greateft religious freedom in the world, they did not find themfelves better fatisfied than they had been in England. There they were tolerated indeed, but watched; their zeal began to have dangerous languors for want of oppofition; and being without power or confequence, they grew tired of the indolent fecurity of their fanctuary; they chofe to remove to a place where they fhould fee no fuperior; and therefore they fent an agent to England, who agreed with the council of Plymouth for a tract of land in America, within their jurifdiction, to fettle in, after they had obtained from the king a privilege to do fo. The Plymouth council was a company, who by their charter had not only all the coaft of North America from Nova Scotia to the Southern parts of Carolina, (the whole country being then diftinguifhed by the names of South and North Virginia) as a fcene for their exclufive trade; but they had the entire property of the foil befides.

This colony eftablifhed itfelf at a place which they called New Plymouth. They were but few in number; they landed in a bad feafon; and they were not at all fupported but from their private funds. The winter was premature, and terribly cold. The country was try was all covered with wood, and afforded very little for the refreshment of persons sickly with such a voyage, or for sustenance of an infant people. Near half of them perished by the scurvy, by want, and the severity of the climate; but they who survived, not dispirited with their losses, nor with the hardships they were still to endure, supported by the vigour which was then the character of Englishmen, and by the satisfaction of finding themselves out of the reach of the spiritual arm, they reduced this savage country to yield them a tolerable livelihood, and by degrees a comfortable subsistence.

This little establishment was made in the year 1621. Several of their brethren in England labouring under the same difficulties, took the same methods of escaping from them. The colony of puritans insensibly increased; but as yet they had not extended themselves much beyond New Plymouth. It was in the year 1629, that the colony began to flourish in such a manner, that they soon became a considerable people. By the close of the ensuing year they had built four towns, Salem, Dorchester, Charles-town, and Boston, which has since become the capital of New England. That enthusiasm which was reversing every thing at home, and which is so dangerous in every settled community, proved of admirable service here. It became a principle of life and vigour, that enabled them to conquer all the difficulties of a savage country. Their exact and sober manners proved a substitute for a proper subordination, and regular form of government, which they had for some time wanted, and the want of which in such a country had otherwise been felt very severely.

And now, not only they who found themselves uneasy at home upon a religious account, but several on account of the then profitable trade of furs and skins, and for the sake of the fishery, were invited to settle in New England. But this colony received its principal assistance from the discontent of several great men of the puritan party, who were its protectors, and who entertained a design of settling amongst them in New England, if they should fail in the measures they were pursuing for establishing the liberty, and reforming the religion of their mother country. They sollicited grants in New England, and were at a great expence in settling them. Amongst these patentees, we see the lords Brook, Say and Seal, the Pelhams, the Hampdens, and the Pyms; the names which afterwards appeared with so much eclat upon a greater stage. It was said that sir Matthew Boynton, sir William Constable, sir Arthur Haslerig, and Oliver Cromwell were actually upon the point of embarking for New England; when archbishop Laud, unwilling that so many objects of his hatred should be removed out of the reach of his power, applied for, and obtained an order from the court to put a stop to these transportations; and thus he kept forcibly from venting itself that virulent humour which he lived to see the destruction of himself, his order, his religion, his master, and the constitution of his country. However, he was not able to prevail so far as to hinder New England from receiving vast reinforcements, as well of the clergy who were deprived of their livings, or not admitted to them for nonconformity, as of such of the laity who adhered to their opinions.

CHAP. III.

Difference in religion, divides the colony. Massachuset. Connecticut. Providence. Spirit of persecution. Persecution of the quakers. Disputes about grace.

THE part of New England called Massachuset's Bay, had now settlements very thick all along the sea shore. Some slips from these were planted in the province of Main and New Hampshire, being torn from the original stock by the religious violence, which was the chief characteristic of the first settlers in New England. The patentees we last mentioned,

mentioned, principally settled upon the river Connecticut, and established a separate and independent government there: some persons having before that fixed themselves upon the borders of this river, who fled from the tyranny arising from the religious differences which were moulded into the first principles of the Plymouth and Massachuset's colonies.

For a considerable time the people of New England had hardly any that deserved the name of a regular form of government. The court took very little care of them. By their charter they were empowerd to establish such an order, and to make such laws as they pleased, provided they were not contrary to the laws of England. A point not easily settled, neither was there any means appointed for settling it. As they who composed the new colonies were generally persons of a contracted way of thinking, and most violent enthusiasts, they imitated the Jewish polity in almost all respects; and adopted the books of Moses as the law of the land. The first laws which they made were grounded upon them, and were therefore very ill suited to the customs, genius, or circumstances of that country, and of those times; for which reason they have since fallen into disuse.

As to religion, it was, as I have said, the puritan. In England this could hardly be considered as a formed sect at the time of their

their emigration, since several who had received episcopal ordination were reckoned to belong to it. But as soon as they found themselves at liberty in America, they fell into a way very little different from the independent mode. Every parish was sovereign within itself. Synods indeed were occasionally called, but they served only to prepare and digest matters, which were to receive their sanction from the approbation of the several churches. The synods could exercise no branch of ecclesiastical jurisdiction, either as to doctrine or to discipline. They had no power of excommunication. They could only refuse to hold communion with those whose principles and practices they disliked. The magistrates assisted in those synods, not only to hear, but to deliberate and determine. From such a form as this, great religious freedom might, one would have imagined, be well expected. But the truth is, they had no idea at all of such a freedom. The very doctrine of any sort of toleration was so odious to the greater part, that one of the first persecutions set up here, was against a small party which arose amongst themselves, who were hardy enough to maintain, that the civil magistrate had no lawful power to use compulsory measures in affairs of religion. After harrassing these people by all the vexatious ways imaginable, they obliged them to fly out of of their jurisdiction. These emigrants settled themselves to the Southward, near Cape Cod, where they formed a new government upon their own principles, and built a town, which they called Providence. This has since made the fourth and smallest, but not the worst inhabited of the New England governments, called Rhode Island, from an island of that name which forms a part of it. As a persecution gave rise to the first settlement of New England, so a subsequent persecution in this colony gave rise to new colonies, and this facilitated the spreading of the people over the country.

If men, merely for the moderation of their sentiments, were exposed to such severe treatment, it was not to be expected that others should escape unpunished. The very first colony had hardly set its foot in America, when discovering that some amongst them were false brethren, and ventured to make use of the common prayer, they found means of making the country so uneasy to them that they were glad to fly back to England.

As soon as they began to think of making laws, I find no less than five about matters of religion; all contrived, and not only contrived, but executed in some respects with so much rigour, that the persecution which drove the puritans out of England, might be considered as great lenity and indulgence in the comparison. For in the first of these laws, they deprive every one who does not communicate with their established church, of the right to his freedom, or a vote in the election of any of their magistrates. In the second, they sentence to banishment any who should oppose the fourth commandment, or deny the validity of infant baptism, or the authority of magistrates. In the third, they condemn quakers to banishment, and make it capital for them to return; and not stopping at the offenders, they lay heavy fines upon all who should bring them into the province, or even harbour them for an hour. In the fourth they provide banishment, and death in case of return, for jesuits and Popish priests of every denomination. In the fifth they decree death to any who shall worship images. After they had provided such a complete code of persecution, they were not long without opportunities of reading bloody lectures upon it. The quakers, warmed with that spirit which animates the beginning of most sects, had spread their doctrines all over the British dominions in Europe, and began at last to spread them with equal zeal in America. The clergy and the magistrates in New England took the alarm; they seized upon some of those people, they set them in the stocks and in the pillory without effect; they scourged, they imprisoned, they banished them; they

treated

treated all those who seemed to commiserate their sufferings with great rigour; but their persecution had no other effect than to inflame their own cruelty and the zeal of the sufferers. The constancy of the quakers under their sufferings begot a pity and esteem for their persons, and an approbation of their doctrines; their proselytes increased; the quakers returned as fast as they were banished; and the fury of the ruling party was raised to such a height, that they proceeded to the most sanguinary extremities. Upon the law they had made, they seized at different times upon five of those who had returned from banishment, condemned and hanged them. It is unknown how far their madness had extended, if an order from the king and council in England about the year 1661 had not interposed to restrain them.

It is a task not very agreeable to insist upon such matters; but in reality, things of this nature form the greatest part of the history of New England, for a long time. They persecuted the anabaptists, who were no inconsiderable body amongst them, with almost an equal severity. In short, this people, who in England could not bear being chastised with rods, had no sooner got free from their fetters than they scourged their fellow refugees with scorpions; though the absurdity, as well as the injustice of such a proceeding in them, might stare them in the face!

One may observe, that men of all persuasions confine the word persecution, and all the ill ideas of injustice and violence which belong to it, solely to those severities which are exercised upon themselves, or upon the party they are inclined to favour. Whatever is inflicted upon others, is a just punishment upon obstinate impiety, and not a restraint upon conscientious differences. The persecution we have ourselves suffered, is a good ground for retaliation against an old enemy; and if one of our friends and fellow sufferers should prove so wicked as to quit our cause, and weaken it by his dissention, he deserves to be punished yet more than the old enemy himself. Besides this, the zealous never fail to draw political inferences from religious tenets, by which they interest the magistrate in the dispute; and then to the heat of a religious fervour is added the fury of a party zeal. All intercourse is cut off between the parties. They lose all knowledge of each other, tho' countrymen and neighbours, and are therefore easily imposed upon with the most absurd stories concerning each other's opinions and practices. They judge of the hatred of the adverse side by their own. Then fear is added to their hatred; and preventive injuries
arise

arise from their fear. The remembrance of the past, the dread of the future, the present ill, will join together to urge them forward to the most violent courses.

Such is the manner of proceeding of religious parties towards each other; and in this respect the New England people are not worse than the rest of mankind, nor was their severity any just matter of reflection upon that mode of religion which they profess. No religion whatsoever, true or false, can excuse its own members, or accuse those of any other upon the score of persecution. The principles which give rise to it are common to all mankind, and they influence them as they are men, and not as they belong to this or that persuasion. In all persuasions the bigots are persecutors; the men of a cool and reasonable piety are favourers of toleration; because the former sort of men not taking the pains to be acquainted with the grounds of their adversaries tenets, conceive them to be so absurd and monstrous, that no man of sense can give into them in good earnest. For which reason they are convinced that some oblique bad motive induces them to pretend to the belief of such doctrines, and to the maintaining of them with obstinacy. This is a very general principle in all religious differences, and it is the corner stone of all persecution.

Besides

Besides the disputes with those of another denomination, the independents were for a long time harrassed with one in the bowels of their own churches. The stale dispute about grace and works produced dissensions, riots, and almost a civil war in the colony. The famous Sir Henry Vane the younger, an enthusiastic, giddy, turbulent man, of a no very good disposition, came hither with some of the adventurers; and rather than remain idle, play'd at small games in New England, where the people had chosen him governor. It is not hard to conceive, how such a man, at the head of such a people, and engaged in such controversy, could throw every thing into confusion. In the very height of this hopeful dispute they had a war upon their hands with some of the Indian nations. Their country was terribly harrassed, and numbers were every day murdered by the incursions of the enemy. All this time they had an army in readiness for action, which they would not suffer to march even to defend their own lives and possessions, because " many of the " officers and soldiers were under a covenant " of works."

CHAP.

CHAP. IV.

The Witchcraft delusion. Great cruelties. The madness ends in the accusation of the magistrates. Reflections.

WHEN the New England puritans began to breathe a little from these dissentions, and had their hands tied up from persecuting the quakers and anabaptists, they fell not long after into another madness of a yet more extraordinary and dangerous kind, which, like some epidemical disease, ran through the whole country, and which is perhaps one of the most extraordinary delusions recorded in history. This tragedy began in the year 1692.

There is a town in New England, which they fanatically called Salem. One Paris was the minister there. He had two daughters troubled with convulsions; which being attended with some of those extraordinary appearances, not unfrequent in such disorders, he imagined they were bewitched. As soon as he concluded upon witchcraft as the cause of the distemper, the next enquiry was how to find out the person who had bewitched them. He cast his eyes upon an Indian servant woman of his own, whom he frequently beat, and used her with such severity, that she at last confessed

confessed herself the witch, and was committed to goal, where she lay for a long time.

The imaginations of the people were not yet sufficiently heated to make a very formal business of this; therefore they were content to discharge her from prison after a long confinement, and to sell her as a slave for her fees.

However, as this example set the discourse about witchcraft afloat, some people, troubled with a similar complaint, began to fancy themselves bewitched too. Persons in an ill state of health are naturally fond of finding out causes for their distempers; especially such as are extraordinary, and call the eyes of the public upon them. There was perhaps something of malice in the affair besides. For one of the first objects whom they fixed upon was Mr. Burroughs, a gentleman who had formerly been minister of Salem; but upon some of the religious disputes which divided the country, he differed with his flock and left them. This man was tried with two others for witchcraft by a special commission of oyer and terminer, directed to some of the gentlemen of the best fortunes, and reputed to be of the best understandings in the country. Before these judges, a piece of evidence was delivered, the most weak and childish, the most repugnant to itself, and to common sense, that perhaps ever was known upon any serious occasion.

casion. Yet by those judges, upon that evidence, and the verdict founded upon it, this minister, a man of a most unexceptionable character, and two others, men irreproachable in their lives, were sentenced to die, and accordingly hanged. Then these victims of the popular madness were stript naked, and their bodies thrown into a pit, half covered with earth, and left to the discretion of birds and wild beasts. Upon the same evidence in a little time after sixteen more suffered death, the greatest part of them dying in the most exemplary sentiments of piety, and with the strongest professions of their innocence. One man refusing to plead, suffered in the cruel manner the law directs on that occasion, by a slow pressure to death.

The imaginations of the people, powerfully affected by these shocking examples, turned upon nothing but the most gloomy and horrid ideas. The most ordinary and innocent actions were metamorphosed into magical ceremonies, and the fury of the people augmented in proportion as this gloom of imagination increased. The flame spread with rage and rapidity into every part of the country. Neither the tenderness of youth, nor the infirmity of age, nor the honour of the sex, nor the sacredness of the ministry, nor the respectable condition of fortune or character, was the least protection. Children of eleven years

years old were taken up for forceries. The women were stripped in the most shameful manner to search them for magical teats. The scorbutic stains common on the skins of old persons, were called the devil's pinches. This was indisputable evidence against them. As such they admitted every idle flying report, and even stories of ghosts, which they honoured with a name, not found in our law books. They called them *Spectral Evidence*.

What these extraordinary testimonies wanted was compleated by the torture, by which a number of these unhappy victims were driven to confess whatever their tormentors thought proper to dictate to them. Some women owned they had been lain with by the devil, and other things equally ridiculous and abominable.

It is not difficult to imagine the deplorable state of this province, when all mens lives depended upon the caprice and folly of diseased and distracted minds; when revenge and malice had a full opportunity of wreaking themselves in a most dreadful and bloody manner, by an instrument that was always in readiness, and to which the public phrenzy gave a certain and dangerous effect. What was a yet worse circumstance, the wretches who suffered the torture, being not more pressed to own themselves guilty than to discover their associates and accomplices, unable to give

give any real account, named people at random, who were immediately taken up, and treated in the same cruel manner upon this extorted evidence. An universal terror and consternation seized upon all. Some prevented accusation, and charged themselves with witchcraft, and so escaped death. Others fled the province; and many more were preparing to fly. The prisons were crouded; people were executed daily; yet the rage of the accusers was as fresh as ever, and the number of the witches and the bewitched increased every hour. A magistrate who had committed forty persons for this crime, fatigued with so disagreeable an employment, and ashamed of the share he had in it, refused to grant any more warrants. He was himself immediately accused of sorcery; and thought himself happy in leaving his family and fortune, and escaping with life out of the province. A jury struck with the affecting manner, and the solemn assurances of innocence of a woman brought before them, ventured to acquit her, but the judges sent them in again; and in an imperious manner forced them to find the woman guilty, and she was hanged immediately.

The magistrates and ministers, whose prudence ought to have been employed in healing this distemper, and assuaging its fury, threw in new combustible matter. They encouraged the accusers; they assisted at the examinations, and they extorted the confessions of witches. None signalized their zeal more upon this occasion than Sir William Phips the governor, a New England man, of the lowest birth, and yet meaner education; who having raised a sudden fortune by a lucky accident, was knighted, and afterwards made governor of the province. Doctor Encrease Mather, and Doctor Cotton Mather, the pillars of the New England church, were equally sanguine. Several of the most popular ministers after twenty executions had been made, addressed Sir William Phips with thanks for what he had done, and with exhortations to proceed in so laudable a work.

The accusers encouraged in this manner did not know where to stop, nor how to proceed. They were at a loss for objects. They began at last to accuse the judges themselves. What was worse, the nearest relations of Mr. Encrease Mather were involved, and witchcraft began even to approach the governor's own family. It was now high time to give things another turn. The accusers were discouraged by authority. One hundred and fifty who lay in prison, were discharged. Two hundred more were under accusation; they were passed over; and those who had received sentence of death, were reprieved, and in due time pardoned. A few cool moments
shewed

shewed them the gross, and stupid error that had carried them away, and which was utterly invisible to them all the while they were engaged in this strange prosecution. They grew heartily ashamed of what they had done. But what was infinitely mortifying, the quakers took occasion to attribute all this mischief to a judgment on them for their persecution. A general fast was appointed; praying God to pardon all the errors of his servants and people in a late tragedy, raised amongst them by Satan and his instruments.

This was the last paroxism of the puritanic enthusiasm in New England. This violent fit carried off so much of that humour, that the people there are now grown somewhat like the rest of mankind in their manners, and have much abated of their persecuting spirit.

It is not an incurious speculation to consider these remarkable sallies of the human mind, out of its ordinary course. Whole nations are often carried away by what would never influence one man of sense. The cause is originally weak, and to be suppressed without great difficulty; but then its weakness prevents any suspicion of the mischief, until it is too late to think of suppressing it at all. In such cases the more weak, improbable, and inconsistent any story is, the more powerful and general is its effect, being helped on by design in some, by folly in others, and kept up by contagion in all. The more extraordinary the design, the more dreadful the crime, the less we examine into the proofs. The charge and the evidence of some things is the same. However, in some time the minds of people cool, and they are astonished how they ever came to be so affected.

CHAP. V.

The situation, climate, &c. of New England. Indian corn described. Cattle of New England.

THE events in the history of New England, their disputes with their governors, the variations in their charters, and their wars with the Indians, afford very little useful or agreeable matter. In their wars there was very little conduct shewn; and though they prevailed in the end, in a manner to the exterpation of that race of people, yet the Indians had always great advantages in the beginning; and the measures of the English to oppose them, were generally injudiciously taken. Their manner too of treating them in the beginning was so indiscreet (for it was in general no worse) as to provoke them as much to those wars, as the French influence has done since that time.

The

The country which we call New England, is in length something less than three hundred miles; at the broadest part it is about two hundred, if we carry it on to those tracts which are possessed by the French; but if we regard the part we have settled, in general, it does not extend any where much above sixty miles from the sea coast.

This country lies between the 41st and 45th degrees of North latitude. Though it is situated almost ten degrees nearer the sun than we are in England, yet the winter begins earlier, lasts longer, and is incomparably more severe than it is with us. The summer again is extremely hot, and more fervently so than in places which lie under the same parallels in Europe. However, both the heat and the cold are now far more moderate, and the constitution of the air in all respects far better than our people found it at their first settlement. The clearing away the woods, and the opening the ground every where, has, by giving a free passage to the air, carried off those noxious vapours which were so prejudicial to the health of the first inhabitants. The temper of the sky is generally both in summer and in winter very steady and serene. Two months frequently pass without the appearance of a cloud. Their rains are heavy and soon over.

The foil of New England is various, but beſt as you approach the Southward. It affords excellent meadows in the low grounds, and very good paſture almoſt every where. They commonly allot at the rate of two acres to the maintenance of a cow. The meadows which they reckon the beſt, yield about a ton of hay by the acre. Some produce two tons, but the hay is rank and four. This country is not very favourable to any of the European kinds of grain. The wheat is ſubject to be blaſted; the barley is an hungry grain, and the oats are lean and chaffy. But the Indian corn, which makes the general food of the loweſt ſort of people, flouriſhes here. This, as it is a ſpecies of grain not ſo univerſally known in England, and as it is that of all others which yields the greateſt increaſe, I ſhall give a ſhort deſcription of it.

This plant, which the native Americans call the Weachin, is known in ſome of the Southern parts of America by the name of maize. The ear is about a ſpan in length, conſiſting of eight rows of the corn, or more, according to the goodneſs of the ground, with about thirty grains in each row. On the top of the grain hangs a ſort of flower, not unlike a taſſel of ſilk, of various colours, white, blue, greeniſh, black, ſpeckled, ſtriped, which gives this corn as it grows a very beautiful appearance. The grain is of all the colours

lours which prevail in the flower, but moſt frequently yellow and white. The ſtalks grow ſix or eight feet high, and are of a conſiderable thickneſs. They are leſs high in New England, and other Northern countries, than in Virginia and thoſe which lie more to the Southward. They are jointed like a cane, and at each of theſe joints ſhoot out a number of leaves like flags, that make very good fodder for the cattle. The ſtalk is full of a juice, of which a ſyrup as ſweet as ſugar has been frequently made.

This grain is generally ſowed in little ſquares, and requires a very attentive cultivation. The ground in which it flouriſhes moſt is light and ſandy, with a ſmall intermixture of loam. About a peck of ſeed is ſufficient for an acre, which at a medium produces about twenty-five buſhels. The New England people not only make bread of this grain, but they malt and brew it into a beer, which is not contemptible. However, the greater part of their beer is made of molaſſes, hopped; with the addition ſometimes of the tops of the ſpruce fir infuſed.

They raiſe in New England, beſides this and other ſpecies of grain, a large quantity of flax, and have made eſſays upon hemp, that have been far from unſucceſsful. An acre of their cow-pen land produces about a ton of this commodity; but the land is pretty ſoon exhauſt-

exhausted. This plant probably requires a climate more uniformly warm than New England; for though the greater part of our hemp is brought to us from Northern ports, yet it is in the more Southerly provinces of Russia, that the best which comes to our market is produced.

Their horned cattle are very numerous in New England, and some of them very large. Oxen have been killed there of eighteen hundred weight. Hogs likewise are numerous, and particularly excellent; and some so large as to weigh twenty-five score. They have besides, a breed of small horses, which are extremely hardy. They pace naturally, though in no very graceful or easy manner, but with such swiftness, and for so long a continuance, as must appear almost incredible to those who have not experienced it. They have a great number of sheep too, and of a good kind. The wool is of a staple sufficiently long, but it is not near so fine as that of England. However, they manufacture a great deal of it very succesfully. I have seen cloths made there, which were of as close and firm a contexture, tho' not so fine, as our best drabs; they were thick, and, as far as I could judge, superior for the ordinary wear of country people, to any thing we make in England.

CHAP.

CHAP. VI.

People of New England. Their numbers. History of the charters of the colonies here, and the forfeiture of some.

THERE are in this country many gentlemen of confiderable landed eftates, which they let to farmers, or manage by their ftewards or overfeers; but the greater part of the people is compofed of a fubftantial yeomanry who cultivate their own freeholds, without a dependence upon any but Providence and their own induftry. Thefe freeholds generally pafs to their children in the way of gavelkind; which keeps them from being almoft ever able to emerge out of their original happy mediocrity. This manner of inheriting has here an additional good effect. It makes the people the more ready to go backward into the uncultivated parts of the country, where land is to be had at an eafy rate and in larger portions. The people by their being generally freeholders, and by their form of government, have a very free, bold, and republican fpirit. In no part of the world are the ordinary fort fo independent, or poffefs fo many of the conveniencies of life; they are ufed from their infancy to the exercife of arms; and they have a militia, which for a militia is by no means contemptible; and certainly if these men were somewhat more regularly trained, and in better subordination, it would be impossible to find in any country, or in any time ancient or modern, an army better constituted than that which New England can furnish. This too is much the best peopled of any of our colonies upon the continent. It is judged that the four provinces which it comprises, contain about three hundred and fifty thousand souls, including a very small number of blacks and Indians; the rest are whites. Douglass, who seems to be well informed in this point, proportions them as follow,

Massachusets bay,	200,000
Connecticut,	100,000
Rhode Island,	30,000
New Hampshire,	24,000
	354,000

These four governments are confederated for their common defence. We have shewn how these several governments have arisen. The most considerable of them for riches and number of people, though not for extent of territory, is Massachusets bay. This province like the others had originally a power of chusing every one of their own magistrates; the governor, the council, the assembly,—all;

and

and of making such laws as they thought proper, without sending them home for the approbation of the crown. But being accused of having abused this freedom, in the latter end of the reign of Charles the second, they were deprived of it by a judgment in a *quo warranto* in the king's bench in England. They remained from that time to the revolution without any charter. Some time after the revolution they received a new one, which though very favourable, was much inferior to the extensive privileges of the former charter, which indeed were too extensive for a colony, and what left little more than a nominal dependence on the mother country, and the crown itself. But now, the governor, lieutenant governor, and the chief places of the law and in the revenue, are in the disposal of the crown; so is the militia; and tho' the council is chosen by the representatives of the people, yet the governor has a negative which gives him an influence, sufficient to preserve the prerogative entire. Appeals for sums above three hundred pounds are admitted to the king and council, and all laws passed here must be remitted to England; where if they do not receive a negative from the crown in three years, they are to be considered as valid, and are to have the effect of laws; which they are to have likewise until the time that the king's resolution is known. But one point has

has been long and resolutely disputed in this colony; the grant of a certain salary to their governor. Many attempts have been made to induce them to this measure; but to no effect. They think a dependence on the people for his salary the most effectual method of restraining the governor from any unpopular acts. To the Massachusets government is united the ancient colony of Plymouth, and the territory which is called Main.

The colony of Connecticut, which lies upon a river of the same name to the South of this province, has preserved its ancient privileges, which are now as considerable as those of Massachusets were formerly. At the time that the charter of the former was attacked, that of this government was threatened with the same fate. But they agreed to submit to the king's pleasure; therefore, no judgment was given against them; and being found in this condition at the revolution, it was judged that they were in full possession of their old charter, and have so continued ever since.

The third and smallest of the provinces which compose New England, is Rhode Island. This consists of a small island of that name, and the old plantation of Providence. These united plantations had a charter the same with that of Connecticut, and they have preserved it by the same method. In this province

province is an unlimited freedom of religion, agreeable to the firſt principles of its foundation; and though very ſmall, it is from thence extremely well peopled.

New Hampſhire, the fourth province, is much the largeſt of them all; but not inhabited in proportion. This is more Northerly for the greater part than any of the reſt. It is a royal government; that is, the crown has the nomination of all the officers of juſtice and of the militia, and the appointment of the council.

CHAP. VII.

Boſton, its harbour. Trade. Ship-building. Diſtillery. Foreign traffic. Reflections on the ſcheme of limiting it. Declenſion of the trade of New England.

THERE is not one of our ſettlements which can be compared in the abundance of people, the number of conſiderable and trading towns, and the manufactures that are carried on in them, to New England. The moſt populous and flouriſhing parts of the mother country hardly make a better appearance. Our provinces to the Southward on this continent are recommendable for the generous warmth of the climate, and a luxuriance of ſoil which naturally throws up a vaſt

variety

variety of beautiful and rich vegetable productions; but New England is the firſt in America, for cultivation, for the number of people, and for the order which reſults from both.

Though there are in all the provinces of New England large towns which drive a conſiderable trade, the only one which can deſerve to be much inſiſted upon in a deſign like ours, is Boſton; the capital of Maſſachuſets bay, the firſt city of New England, and of all North America. This city is ſituated on a peninſula, at the bottom of a fine capacious and ſafe harbour, which is defended from the outrages of the ſea, by a number of iſlands, and rocks which appear above water. It is entered but by one ſafe paſſage; and that is narrow, and covered by the cannon of a regular and very ſtrong fortreſs. The harbour is more than ſufficient for the great number of veſſels, which carry on the extenſive trade of Boſton. At the bottom of the bay is a noble pier, near two thouſand feet in length, along which on the North ſide extends a row of warehouſes. The head of this pier joins the principal ſtreet of the town, which is, like moſt of the others, ſpacious and well built. The town lies at the bottom of the harbour, and forms a very agreeable view. It has a town houſe, where the courts meet, and the exchange is kept, large, and of a very tolerable taſte of architecture. Round the exchange,

are

are a great number of well furnished bookfellers shops, which find employment for five printing presses. There are ten churches within this town; and it contains at least twenty thousand inhabitants.

That we may be enabled to form some judgment of the wealth of this city, we must observe that from Christmas 1747, to Christmas 1748, five hundred vessels cleared out from this port only, for a foreign trade; and four hundred and thirty were entered inwards; to say nothing of coasting and fishing vessels, both of which are extremely numerous, and said to be equal in number to the others. Indeed the trade of New England is great, as it supplies a large quantity of goods from within itself; but it is yet greater, as the people of this country are in a manner the carriers for all the colonies of North America and the West-Indies, and even for some parts of Europe. They may be considered in this respect as the Dutch of America.

The commodities which the country yields are principally masts and yards, for which they contract largely with the royal navy; pitch, tar and turpentine; staves, lumber; boards; all sorts of provisions, beef, pork, butter and cheese, in large quantities; horses and live cattle; Indian corn and pease; cyder, apples, hemp and flax. Their peltry trade is not very considerable. They have a very noble
cod

cod fishery upon their coast, which employs a vast number of their people; they are enabled by this to export annually above thirty-two thousand quintals of choice cod fish, to Spain, Italy, and the Mediterranean, and about nineteen thousand quintals of the refuse sort to the West-Indies, as food for the negroes, The quantity of spirits, which they distil in Boston from the molasses they bring in from all parts of the West-Indies, is as surprising as the cheap rate at which they vend it, which is under two shillings a gallon. With this they supply almost all the consumption of our colonies in North America, the Indian trade there, the vast demands of their own and the Newfoundland fishery, and in great measure those of the African trade; but they are more famous for the quantity and cheapness, than for the excellency of their rum.

They are almost the only one of our colonies which have much of the woollen and linen manufactures. Of the former they have nearly as much as suffices for their own cloathing. It is a close and strong, but a coarse stubborn sort of cloth. A number of presbyterians from the North of Ireland, driven thence, as it is said, by the severity of their landlords, from an affinity in religious sentiments chose New England as their place of refuge. Those people brought with them
their

their skill in the linen manufactures, and meeting with very large encouragement, they exercised it to the great advantage of this colony. At present they make large quantities, and of a very good kind; their principal settlement is in a town, which in compliment to them is called Londonderry. Hats are made in New England which in a clandestine way find a good vent in all the other colonies. The setting up these manufactures has been in a great measure a matter necessary to them; for as they have not been properly encouraged in some staple commodity, by which they might communicate with their mother country, while they were cut off from all other resources, they must either have abandoned the country, or have found means of employing their own skill and industry to draw out of it the necessaries of life. The same necessity, together with their convenience for building and manning ships, has made them the carriers for the other colonies.

The business of ship-building is one of the most considerable which Boston or the other sea-port towns in New England carry on. Ships are sometimes built here upon commission; but frequently, the merchants of New England have them constructed upon their own account; and loading them with the produce of the colony, naval stores, fish, and fish-oil principally, they send them out upon a trading

ding voyage to Spain, Portugal, or the Mediterranean, where having difpofed of their cargo they make what advantage they can by freight, until fuch time as they can fell the veffel herfelf to advantage, which they feldom fail to do in a reafonable time. They receive the value of the veffel, as well as of the freight of the goods, which from time to time they carried, and of the cargo with which they failed originally, in bills of exchange upon London; for as the people of New England have no commodity to return for the value of above a hundred thoufand pounds, which they take in various forts of goods from England, but fome naval ftores, and thofe in no great quantities, they are obliged to keep the balance fomewhat even by this circuitous commerce, which though not carried on with Great Britain nor with Britifh veffels, yet centers in its profits, where all the money which the colonies can make in any manner, muft center at laft.

I know that complaints have been made of this trade, principally becaufe the people of New England, not fatisfied with carrying out their own produce, become carriers for the other colonies, particularly for Virginia and Maryland, from whom they take tobacco, which, in contempt of the act of navigation, they carry directly to the foreign market. Where, not having the duty and accumulated charges to which the Britifh merchant is liable

to

to pay, they in a manner wholly out him of the trade. Again, our sugar colonies complain as loudly, that the vast trade which New England drives in lumber, live stock and provisions with the French and Dutch sugar islands, particularly with the former, enables these islands, together with the internal advantages they possess, greatly to undersell the English plantations. That the returns which the people of New England make from these islands being in sugar, or the productions of sugar, syrups and molasses, the rum which is thence distilled prevents the sale of our West-India rum. That this trade proves doubly disadvantageous to our sugar islands; first, as it enables the French to sell their sugars cheaper than they could otherwise afford to do; and then as it finds them a market for their molasses, and other refuse of sugars, for which otherwise they could find no market at all; because rum interferes with brandy, a considerable manufacture of Old France.

These considerations were the ground of a complaint made by the islands to the legislature in England some years ago. They desired that the exportation of lumber, &c. to the French colonies, and the importation of sugars and molasses from thence, might be entirely prohibited. This was undoubtedly a very nice point to settle. On one hand, the growth of the French West-Indies was manifest and alarming, and it was not to be thought that the French would ever wink at this trade, if it had not been of the greatest advantage to them, On the other hand, the Northern colonies declared, that if they were deprived of so great a branch of their trade, it must necessiate them to the establishment of manufactures. For if they were cut off from their foreign trade, they never could purchase in England the many things for the use or the ornament of life, which they have from thence. Besides this, the French deprived of the provision and lumber of New England, must of necessity take every measure to be supplied from their own colonies, which would answer their purposes better, if they could accomplish it, at the same time that it would deprive the New England people of a large and profitable branch of their trade.

These points, and many more, were fully discussed upon both sides. The legislature took a middle course. They did not entirely prohibit the carrying of lumber to the French islands, but they laid a considerable duty upon whatever rum, sugars or molasses they should import from thence, to enhance by this means the price of lumber, and other necessaries to the French, and by laying them under difficulties, to set the English sugar plantations in

some

some measure upon an equal footing with theirs.

This was undoubtedly a very prudent regulation. For though it was urged, that the Missisippi navigation was so bad, that there was no prospect that the French could ever be supplied with lumber and provisions from thence; and that there were no snows in Louisiana, the melting of which might facilitate the transportation of lumber into that river, yet it was by no means safe to trust to that, so as utterly to destroy a trade of our own, which employed so much shipping, and so many sailors. Because we have a thousand instances, wherein the driving people to the last streights, and putting them under the tuition of such a master as absolute necessity, has taught them inventions, and excited them to an industry, which have compassed things as much regretted at last, as they were unforeseen at first.

Though no great snows fall in the Southern parts of Louisiana, yet to the Northward a great deal falls, and not only the Missisippi, but the number of other great rivers which it receives, overflow annually, and they can be in no want of timber convenient enough to navigation. And though the passage to the French islands be for such a great way to the windward, as to bring them these commodities in a more tedious manner, and at a dearer rate,

rate, is it not much better that they should have them cheap from us than dear from themselves? Nor perhaps would even this difficulty, which is indeed much less than it is represented, bring down the French to the par of our sugar colonies, loaded as they are with taxes, groaning under the pressure of many grievances, and deformed by an infinite multitude of abuses and enormities; nor can they with reason or justice hope for a cure of the evils which they suffer, partly from errors of their own, and partly from mistakes in England, at the expence of the trade of their sister colonies on the continent of America, who are entirely guiltless of their sufferings; nor is it by restraints on their trade, but by an effectual and judicious encouragement of their own, that they can hope to remedy these evils, and rival the French establishments.

The French, in permitting us to supply them, it is true, give us a proof that they have advantages from this trade; but this is no proof at all that we derive none from it; for on that supposition no trade could be mutually beneficial. Nor is it at all certain, as it has been suggested, that if we left their refuse of sugars upon their hands, that they could turn them to no profit. If the council of commerce could be made to see distinctly that this trade could not prejudice the sale of their brandy,

brandy, and would only make the trade of rum change hands, as the case probably would be; and if they could shew, as they might, what a loss it must be to them entirely to throw away a considerable part of the produce of their lands, and which was formerly so valuable to them, there is no doubt but the court would give sufficient encouragement to their own plantations to distil rum, and to vend it in such a manner as might the least prejudice the brandies of France; and then, instead of sending us molasses, as they could distil the spirit far cheaper than our islands, they would send us the spirit itself; and we may know by experience, especially in that part of the world, how insufficient all regulations are to prevent a counterband, which would be so gainful to particulars.

After all, are we certain, that the French would trust for the supply of their islands to Louisiana, or to the precarious supplies from Canada? would they not redouble their application, now made necessary, to Cape Breton? what experiments would they not make in Cayenne for the timber trade? they would certainly try every method, and probably would succeed in some of their trials. Restraints upon trade are nice things; and ought to be well considered. Great care ought to be taken in all such how we sacrifice the interests of one part of our territories to those of another; and it would be a mistake of the

most

most fatal consequence, if we came to think that the shipping, seamen, commodities, or wealth of the British colonies, were not effectually the shipping, seamen, and wealth of Great Britain herself. Sentiments of another kind have frequently done us mischief.

The general plan of our management with regard to the trade of our colonies, methinks, ought to be, to encourage in every one of them some separate and distinct articles, such as not interfering, might enable them to trade with each other, and all to trade to advantage with their mother country. And then, where we have rivals in any branch of the trade carried on by our colonies, to enable them to send their goods to the foreign market directly; using at the same time the wife precaution which the French put in practice, to make the ships so employed take the English ports in their way home; for our great danger is, that they should in that case make their returns in foreign manufactures, against which we cannot guard too carefully. This, and that they should not go largely into manufactures interfering with ours, ought to be the only points at which our restrictions should aim. These purposes ought not to be compassed by absolute prohibitions and penalties, which would be unpolitical and unjust, but by the way of diversion, by encouraging them to fall into such things as find a demand with ourselves

selves at home. By this means Great Britain and all its dependencies will have a common intereft, they will mutually play into each other's hands, and the trade fo difperfed, will be of infinitely more advantage to us, than if all its feveral articles were produced and manufactured within ourfelves.

I venture on thefe hints concerning reftraints on trade, becaufe in fact that of New England rather wants to be fupported than to be checked by fuch reftraints. Its trade in many of its branches is clearly on the decline; and this circumftance ought to intereft us deeply; for very valuable is this colony, if it never fent us any thing, nor took any thing from us, as it is the grand barrier of all the reft; and as it is the principal magazine which fupplies our Weft-Indies, from whence we draw fuch vaft advantages. That this valuable colony is far from advancing, will appear clearly from the ftate of one of the principal branches of its trade, that of fhip-building, for four years. In the year 1738 they built at Bofton forty-one topfail veffels, burden in all 6324 tons; in 1743 only thirty; in 46 but twenty; in 49 they were reduced to fifteen, making in the whole but 2450 tons of fhipping; in fuch a time an aftonifhing declenfion! How it has been fince I have not fufficient information; but allowing that the decline has ceafed here, yet this is furely fufficient to set us upon the nicest enquiry into the cause of that decay, and the most effectual measures to retrieve the affairs of so valuable a province; particularly, if by any ill-judged or ill-intended schemes, or by any misgovernment this mischief has happened them.

CHAP. VIII.

New York, New Jersey, and Pensylvania, Description of their situation, &c. Short account of their settlement.

IT is not certainly known at what time the Swedes and Dutch made their first establishment in North America; but it was certainly posterior to our settlement in Virginia, and prior to that of New England. The Swedes, who were no considerable naval power, had hardly fixt the rudiments of a colony there than they deserted it. The inhabitants, without protection or assistance, were glad to enter into a coalition with the Dutch that had settled there upon a better plan, and to submit to the government of the States. The whole tract possessed or claimed by the two nations, whose two colonies were now grown into one, extended from the 38th to the 41st degree of latitude, all along the sea coast. They called it Nova Belgia, or New Netherlands. It continued in their hands until the reign of Charles

the

the second. The Dutch war then breaking out, in the year 1664 Sir Robert Car with three thousand men was sent to reduce it, which he did with so little resistance, as not to gain him any great honour by the conquest. A little after, the Dutch by way of reprisal fell upon our colony of Surinam in South America, and conquered it after much the same opposition that we met in the New Netherlands. By the treaty of peace which was signed at Breda, in 1667, it was agreed that things should remain in the state they were at that time; Surinam to the Dutch, the New Netherlands to the English. At that time, this was looked upon by many as a bad exchange; but it now appears, that we have made an excellent bargain; for to say nothing of the great disadvantage of having our colonies, as it were, cut in two by the intervention of a foreign territory; this is now one of the best peopled and richest parts of our plantations, extremely useful to the others, and making very valuable returns to the mother country; whereas Surinam is comparatively a place of very small consequence, very unhealthy, and by no art to be made otherwise.

The New Netherlands were not long in our possession before they were divided into distinct provinces, and laid aside their former appellation. The North-East part which joined New England, was called New York,

in

in compliment to the duke of York, who had at firſt the grant of the whole territory. This province runs up to the Northward on both ſides of the river Hudſon, for about two hundred miles into the country of the Five Nations or Iroquois; but it is not in any part above forty or fifty miles wide. It comprehends within its limits Long Iſland, which lies to the South of Connecticut, and is an iſland inferior to no part of America in excellent ground for the paſturage of horſes, oxen, and ſheep, or the plentiful produce of every ſort of grain.

The part of Nova Belgia, which lay along the ocean, between that and the river Delawar, from the Southern part of New York quite down to Maryland, was granted to Sir George Carteret and others, and called New Jerſey from him, becauſe he had, as the family ſtill has, eſtates in the iſland of that name. This province is bounded upon the Weſt by the river Delawar, which divides it from Penſylvania. It is in length about one hundred and fifty miles, or thereabouts, and about fifty in breadth.

Penſylvania, which lies between New York, New Jerſey, and Maryland, and only communicates with the ſea by the mouth of the river Delawar, is in length about two hundred and fifty miles, and in breadth two hundred. This territory was granted to the famous Mr. William

William Pen, the fon of Sir William Pen the admiral, in the year 1680.

The climate and foil in the three provinces of New York, New Jerfey, and Penfylvania, admits of no very remarkable difference. In all thefe, and indeed in all our North American colonies, the land near the fea is in general low, flat and marfhy; at a confiderable diftance from the fea it fwells into little hills, and then into great even ridges of mountains, which hold their courfe, for the moft part, North-Eaft, and South-Weft. The foil throughout thefe three provinces is in general extremely fruitful; abounding not only in its native grain the Indian corn, but in all fuch as have been naturalized there from Europe. Wheat in fuch abundance, and of fo excellent a quality, that few parts of the world, for the tract which is cultivated, exceed it in the one or the other of thefe particulars; nor in barley, oats, rye, buck-wheat, and every fort of grain which we have here. They have a great number of horned cattle, horfes, fheep, and hogs. All our European poultry abound there; game of all kinds is wonderfully plenty; deer of feveral fpecies; hares of a kind peculiar to America, but inferior in relifh to ours; wild turkies of a vaft fize, and equal goodnefs; a beautiful fpecies of pheafants, only found in this country. Every fpecies of herbs or roots which we force in our gardens,

grow

grow here with great ease; and every species of fruit; but some, as those of peaches and melons, in far greater perfection.

Their forests abound in excellent timber, the oak, the ash, the beech, the chesnut, the cedar, the walnut, the cypress, the hickory, the sassafras, and the pine. In all parts of our plantations, comprehending New York to the Northward, quite to the Southern extremity, the woods are full of wild vines of three or four species, all different from those we have in Europe. But whether from some fault in their nature, or in the climate, or the soil where they grow, or what is much more probable, from a fault in the planters, they have yet produced no wine that deserves to be mentioned. It may be remarked in general of the timber of these provinces, that it is not so good for shipping as that of New England and Nova Scotia. The further southward you go, the timber becomes less compact, and rives easily; which property, as it makes it more useful for staves, renders it less serviceable for ships.

They raise in all these provinces, but much the most largely in Pensylvania, great quanties of flax; hemp is a promising article. Nor are they deficient in minerals. In New York a good deal of iron is found. In New Jersey a very rich copper mine has been opened.

opened. There is no manner of doubt but in time, when the people come to multiply sufficiently, and experience and want have made them ingenious in opening resources for trade, these colonies will become as remarkable for useful metals as they now are for grain. These three provinces, as are all those we have in North America, are extremely well watered. They have however observed in New England, that as they clear the country, a vast number of little brooks are quite lost, and the mills upon them by this loss rendered useless. They even observe, that this cutting down the woods has affected the river Connecticut itself, the largest in New England, and that it has grown distinguishably shallower. I do not know whether the same remark has been made in Pensylvania and New York. But whatever they have lost in water, which, where there is such a plenty, is no great loss, has been amply compensated by the great salubrity of the air, which has arisen from the cultivation of the country. At present those I describe are for the greater part as healthy as can be wished.

As the climate and soil of the provinces of New York, New Jersey, and Pensylvania, are with a very little difference the same, so there is no difference in the commodities in which they trade, which are wheat, flour, barley, oats, Indian corn, peas, beef, pork, cheese, butter, cyder, beer, flax, hemp and flax-seed,

linseed

linseed oil, furs and deer-skins, staves, lumber, and iron. Their markets are the same with those which the people of New England use; and these colonies have a share in the logwood trade, and that which is carried on with the Spanish and French plantations.

CHAP. IX.

City of New York. Its flourishing trade. Albany. The Indian trade there. The Iroquois or Six Nations.

THE province of New York has two cities; the first is called by the name of the province itself. It was denominated New Amsterdam when the Dutch possessed it, but it has changed its name along with its masters. This city is most commodiously situated for trade, upon an excellent harbour, in an island called Manahatton, about fourteen miles long, though not above one or two broad. This island lies just in the mouth of the river Hudson, which discharges itself here after a long course. This is one of the noblest rivers in America. It is navigable upwards of two hundred miles. The tide flows one hundred and fifty.

The city of New York contains upwards of two thousand houses, and above twelve thousand inhabitants, the descendants of Dutch and English.

English. It is well and commodiously built, extending a mile in length, and about half that in breadth, and has a very good aspect from the sea; but it is by no means properly fortified. The houses are built of brick in the Dutch taste; the streets not regular, but clean and well paved. There is one large church built for the church of England worship; and three others, a Dutch, a French, and a Lutheran. The town has a very flourishing trade, and in which great profits are made. The merchants are wealthy, and the people in general most comfortably provided for, and with a moderate labour. From the year 1749 to 1750 two hundred and thirty-two vessels have been entered in this port, and two hundred and eighty-six cleared outwards. In these vessels were shipped six thousand seven hundred and thirty-one tons of provisions, chiefly flour, and a vast quantity of grain; of which I have no particular account. In the year 1755 the export of flax seed to Ireland amounted to 12,528 hogsheads. The inhabitants are between eighty and an hundred thousand; the lower class easy; the better rich, and hospitable; great freedom of society; and the entry to foreigners made easy by a general toleration of all religious persuasions. In a word, this province yields to no part of America in the healthfulness of its air, and the fertility of its soil. It is much superior in the

great

great convenience of water carriage, which speedily and at the slightest expence carries the product of the remotest farms to a certain and profitable market.

Upon the river Hudson, about one hundred and fifty miles from New York, is Albany; a town of not so much note for its number of houses or inhabitants, as for the great trade which is carried on with the Indians, and indeed by connivance with the French for the use of the same people. This trade takes off a great quantity of coarse woollen goods, such as strouds and duffils; and with these, guns, hatchets, knives, hoes, kettles, powder and shot; besides shirts and cloaths ready made, and several other articles. Here it is that the treaties and other transactions between us and the Iroquois Indians are negotiated.

This nation, or combination of Five nations, united by an ancient and inviolable league amongst themselves, were the oldest, the most steady, and most effectual ally we have found amongst the Indians. This people, by their unanimity, firmness, military skill, and policy, have raised themselves to be the greatest and most formidable power in all America; they have reduced a vast number of nations, and brought under their power a territory twice as large as the kingdom of France; but they have not increased their subjects in proportion. As their manner of warring is implacable and
barbarous,

barbarous, they reign the lords of a prodigious desert, inhabited only by a few scattered insignificant tribes, whom they have permitted to live out of a contempt of their power, and who are all in the lowest state of subjection. And yet this once mighty and victorious nation, though it has always used the policy of incorporating with itself a great many of the prisoners they make in war, is in a very declining condition. About sixty years ago it was computed, that they had ten thousand fighting men; at this day they cannot raise upwards of fifteen hundred. So much have wars, epidemical diseases, and the unnatural union of the vices of civilized nations with the manners of savages, reduced this once numerous people. But they are not only much lessened at this day in their numbers, but in their disposition to employ what numbers they have left in our service. Amongst other neglects, which I have no pleasure in mentioning, and no hopes of seeing amended, this of inattention, or worse treatment of the Indians, is one, and a capital one. The Iroquois have lately had three other nations added to their confederacy, so that they ought now to be considered as eight; and the whole confederacy seems much more inclined to the French interest than ours.

CHAP. X.

New Jersey. Its trade; and inhabitants.

NEW Jersey, by the perpetual disputes which subsisted between the people and the proprietaries, whilst it continued a proprietary government, was kept for a long time in a very feeble state; but within a few years it has begun to reap some of the advantages which it might have had earlier from the proper management of so fine a province and so advantageous a situation. They raise very great quantities of grain at present, and are increased to near sixty thousand souls; but they have yet no town of any consequence. Perth Amboy, which is their capital, has not upwards of two hundred houses; and though this town has a very fine harbour, capable of receiving and securing ships of great burden, yet as the people of New Jersey have been used to send their produce to the markets of New York and Philadelphia, to which they are contiguous, they find it hard, as it always is in such cases, to draw the trade out of the old channel; for there the correspondencies are fixed, the method of dealing established, credits given, and a ready market for needy dealers, who in all countries are sufficiently numerous; so that the trade of this town, which is the only town of any trade worth notice in New Jerſey, is ſtill inconſiderable; in the year 1751, only forty-one veſſels have entered inwards, and only thirty-eight cleared out, in which were exported ſix thouſand four hundred and twenty-four barrels of flour; one hundred and ſixty-eight thouſand weight of bread; three hundred and fourteen barrels of beef and pork; ſeventeen thouſand nine hundred and forty-one buſhels of grain; fourteen thouſand weight of hemp; with ſome butter, hams, beer, flax-ſeed, bar-iron, and lumber.

CHAP. XI.

Account of William Pen. The principles on which he ſettled the colony. His death.

I Find it of late a notion pretty current, that proprietary governments are a ſort of check to the growth of the colonies which they ſuperintend. It is certain, that abuſes have been, and ſtill do ſubſiſt in that ſpecies of government; and abuſes of as bad a kind may, I believe, be found by perſons of no great penetration in all our governments; but if there were any truth in this obſervation, the province of Penſylvania would prove an illuſtrious exception to it.

William Pen in his capacity of a divine, and of a moral writer, is certainly not of the

firſt

first rank; and his works are of no great estimation, except amongst his own people; but in his capacity of a legislator, and the founder of so flourishing a commonwealth, he deserves great honour amongst all mankind; a commonwealth, which in the space of about seventy years, from a beginning of a few hundreds of refugees and indigent men, has grown to be a numerous and flourishing people; a people who from a perfect wilderness have brought their territory to a state of great cultivation, and filled it with wealthy and populous towns; and who in the midst of a fierce and lawless race of men, have preserved themselves with unarmed hands and passive principles, by the rules of moderation and justice, better than any other people has done by policy and arms. For Mr. Pen, when for his father's services, and by his own interest at court, he obtained the inheritance of this country and its government, saw that he could make the grant of value to him only by making the country as agreeable to all people, as ease and good government could make it. To this purpose he began by purchasing the soil, at a very low rate indeed, from the original possessors, to whom it was of little use. By this cheap act of justice at the beginning, he made all his dealings for the future the more easy, by prepossessing the Indians with a favourable opinion of him and his designs. The other

other part of his plan, which was to people this country, after he had secured the possession of it, he saw much facilitated by the uneasiness of his brethren the quakers in England, who refusing to pay tythes and other church dues, suffered a great deal from the spiritual courts. Their high opinion of and regard for the man who was an honour to their new church, made them the more ready to follow him over the vast ocean into an untried climate and country. Neither was he himself wanting in any thing which could encourage them. For he expended large sums in transporting and finding them in all necessaries; and not aiming at a sudden profit, he disposed of his land at a very light purchase. But what crowned all, was that noble charter of privileges, by which he made them as free as any people in the world; and which has since drawn such vast numbers of so many different persuasions, and such various countries, to put themselves under the protection of his laws. He made the most perfect freedom, both religious and civil, the basis of this establishment; and this has done more towards the settling of the province and towards the settling of it in a strong and permanent manner, than the wisest regulations could have done upon any other plan. All persons who profess to believe one God, are freely tolerated; those who believe in Jesus Christ, of whatever denomination, are not excluded from employments and posts.

This great man lived to see an extensive country called after his own name; he lived to see it peopled by his own wisdom, the people free and flourishing, and the most flourishing people in it of his own persuasion; he lived to lay the foundations of a splendid and wealthy city; he lived to see it promise every thing from the situation which he himself had chosen, and the encouragement which he himself had given it; he lived to see all this, but he died in the Fleet prison.

It is but just, that in such a subject we should allot a little room, to do honour to those great men, whose virtue and generosity have contributed to the peopling of the earth, and to the freedom and happiness of mankind; who have preferred the interest of a remote posterity, and times unknown, to their own fortunes, and to the quiet and security of their own lives. Now Great Britain, and all America, reap great benefits from his labours and his losses; and his posterity have a vast estate out of the quit-rents of that province, whose establishment was the ruin of their predecessor's moderate fortune.

CHAP.

CHAP. XII.

Inhabitants of Penſylvania. Variety of nations and religions there. Pacific principles of the quakers. Reflections on the preſent ſtate of affairs there.

PENSYLVANIA is inhabited by upwards of two hundred and fifty thouſand people, half of whom are Germans, Swedes or Dutch. Here you ſee the Quakers, churchmen, calviniſts, lutherans, catholics, methodiſts, meniſts, moravians, independents, the anabaptiſts, and the dumplers, a ſort of German ſect that live in ſomething like a religious ſociety, wear long beards, and a habit reſembling that of friars; in ſhort, the diverſity of people, religions, nations, and languages here, is prodigious, and the harmony in which they live together, no leſs edifying. For though every man who wiſhes well to religion, is ſorry to ſee the diverſity which prevails, and would by all humane and honeſt methods endeavour to prevent it; yet when once the evil has happened, when there is no longer an union of ſentiments, it is glorious to preſerve at leaſt an union of affections; it is a beautiful proſpect, to ſee men take and give an equal liberty; to ſee them live, if not as belonging to the ſame church, yet

yet to the same christian religion; and if not to the same religion, yet to the same great fraternity of mankind. I do not observe, that the quakers, who had, and who still have in a great measure, the power in their hands, have made use of it in any sort to persecute; except in the single case of George Keith, whom they first imprisoned, and then banished out of the province. This Keith was originally a minister of the church of England, then a quaker, and afterwards returned to his former ministry. But whilst he remained with the friends, he was a most troublesome and litigious man; was for pushing the particularities of quakerism to yet more extravagant lengths, and for making new refinements, even where the most enthusiastic thought they had gone far enough; which rash and turbulent conduct raised such a storm, as shook the church, he then adhered to, to the very foundations.

This little sally into intollerance, as it is a single instance, and with great provocation, ought by no means to be imputed to the principles of the quakers, considering the ample and humane latitude they have allowed in all other respects. It was certainly a very right policy to encourage the importation of foreigners into Pensylvania, as well as into our other colonies. By this we are great gainers without any diminution of the inhabitants of

Great

Great Britain. But it has been frequently observed, and as it should seem, very justly complained of, that they are left still foreigners, and likely to continue so for many generations; as they have schools taught, books printed, and even the common news paper in their own language; by which means, and that they possess large tracts of the country, without any intermixture of English, there is no appearance of their blending and becoming one people with us. This certainly is a great irregularity, and the greater, as these foreigners by their industry, frugality, and a hard way of living, in which they greatly exceed our people, have in a manner thrust them out in several places; so as to threaten the colony with the danger of being wholly foreign in language, manners, and perhaps even inclinations. In the year 1750, were imported into Pensylvania and its dependencies four thousand three hundred and seventeen Germans, whereas of British and Irish, but one thousand arrived; a considerable number, if it was not so vastly overbalanced by that of the foreigners.

 I do by no means think that this sort of transplantations ought to be discouraged; I only observe along with others, that the manner of their settlement ought to be regulated, and means sought to have them naturalized in reality.

The

The prefent troubles have very unhappily reverfed the fyftem fo long purfued, and with fuch great fuccefs in this part of the world. The Penfylvanians have fuffered feverely by the incurfions of the favage Americans as well as their neighbours; but the quakers could not be prevailed upon, by what did not directly affect thofe of their own communion, (for they were out of the way of mifchief in the more fettled parts,) to relinquifh their pacific principles; for which reafon a confiderable oppofition, in which, however, we muft do the quakers the juftice to obferve they were not unanimous, was made both within their affembly, as well as without doors, againft granting any money to carry on the war; and the fame, or a more vigorous oppofition, was made againft paffing a militia bill. A bill of this kind has at length paffed, but fcarcely fuch as the circumftances of the country, and the exigencies of the times required. It may perhaps appear an error, to have placed fo great part of the government in the hands of men, who hold principles directly oppofite to its end and defign. As a peaceable, induftrious, honeft people, the quakers cannot be too much cherifhed; but furely they cannot themfelves complain, that when by their opinions they make themfelves fheep, they fhould not be entrufted with the office, fince they have not the nature of dogs.

CHAP.

CHAP. XIII.

Description of Philadelphia. Its trade. Number of people in Penſylvania. Its flouriſhing condition. Few negroes there.

THERE are ſo many good towns in the province of Penſylvania, even exceeding the capitals of ſome other provinces, that nothing could excuſe our paſſing them by, had not Philadelphia drawn our attention wholly to itſelf. This city ſtands upon a tongue of land, immediately at the confluence of two fine rivers, the Delawar and the Schulkil. It is diſpoſed in the form of an oblong, deſigned to extend two miles from river to river; but the buildings do not extend above a mile and an half on the Weſt ſide of Delawar in length, and not more than half a mile where the town is broadeſt. The longeſt ſtretch when the original plan can be fully executed, is to compoſe eight parallel ſtreets, all of two miles in length; theſe are to be interſected by ſixteen others, each in length a mile, broad, ſpacious, and even; with proper ſpaces left for the public buildings, churches, and market-places. In the center is a ſquare of ten acres, round which moſt of the public buildings are diſpoſed. The two principal ſtreets of the city are each one hundred feet wide, and

and most of the houses have a small garden and orchard; from the rivers are cut several canals, equally agreeable and beneficial. The kays are spacious and fine; the principal kay is two hundred feet wide, and to this a vessel of five hundred tons may lay her broadside. The warehouses are large, numerous and commodious, and the docks for ship-building every way well adapted to their purposes. A great number of vessels have been built here; twenty have been upon the stocks at a time. This city contains, exclusive of warehouses and outhouses, about two thousand houses; most of them of brick, and well built; it is said there are several of them worth four or five thousand pounds. The inhabitants are now about thirteen thousand.

There are in this city a great number of very wealthy merchants; which is no way surprising, when one considers the great trade which it carries on with the English, French, Spanish and Dutch colonies in America; with the Azores, the Canaries, and the Madeira islands; with Great Britain and Ireland; with Spain, Portugal and Holland, and the great profits which are made in many branches of this commerce. Besides the quantity of all kinds of the produce of this province which is brought down the rivers Delawar and Schulkil (the former of which is navigable for vessels of one sort or other more than two hundred miles above Philadelphia,) the Dutch employ between eight and nine thousand waggons, drawn each by four horses, in bringing the product of their farms to this market. In the year 1749, three hundred and three vessels entered inwards at this port, and two hundred and ninety-one cleared outwards. There are at the other ports of this province custom-house officers, but the foreign trade in these places is not worth notice.

The city of Philadelphia, though, as it may be judged, far from compleating the original plan; yet so far as it is built, it is carried on conformable to it, and increases in the number and beauty of its buildings every day. And as for the province, of which this city is the capital, there is no part of British America in a more growing condition. In some years more people have transported themselves into Pensylvania, than into all the other settlements together. In 1729, six thousand two hundred and eight persons came to settle here as passengers or servants, four fifths of whom at least were from Ireland. In short, this province has increased so greatly from the time of its first establishment, that lands were given by Mr. Pen the founder of the colony at the rate of twenty pounds for a thousand acres, reserving only a shilling every hundred acres for quit-rent; and this in some

some of the best situated parts of the province; but now at a great distance from navigation, land is granted at twelve pounds the hundred acres, and a quit-rent of four shillings reserved; and the land which is near Philadelphia, rents for twenty shillings the acre. In many places, and at the distance of several miles from that city, land sells for twenty years purchase.

The Pensylvanians are an industrious and hardy people; they are most of them substantial, though but a few of the landed people can be cousidered as rich; but they are all well lodged, well fed, and, for their condition, well clad too; and this at the more easy rate, as the inferior people manufacture most of their own wear both linens and woollens. There are but few blacks, not in all the fortieth part of the people of the province.

CHAP. XIV.

Situation, &c. of Virginia. Conveniency of its rivers for navigation. Beasts and birds of the country. The opossum.

THE whole country which the English now possess in North America, was at first called Virginia; but by parcelling of several portions of it into distinct grants and governments, the country which still bears the name, is now reduced to that tract which has the river Potowmack upon the North; the bay of Chesapeak upon the East; and Carolina upon the South. To the Westward the grants extend it to the South-Sea; but their planting goes no farther than the great Allegany mountains, which boundaries leave this province in length two hundred and forty miles, and in breadth about two hundred, lying between the fifty-fifth and fortieth degrees of North latitude.

The whole face of this country is so extremely low towards the sea, that when you are come even within fifteen fathom soundings you can hardly distinguish land from the mast head. However, all this coast of America has one useful particularity, that you know your distance exactly by the soundings, which uniformly and gradually diminish as you approach the land. The trees appear as if they rose out of the water, and afford the stranger a very uncommon, and not a disagreeable view. In sailing to Virginia or Maryland, you pass a streight between two points of land, called the Capes of Virginia, which opens a passage into the bay of Chesapeak, one of the largest and safest bays perhaps in the world; for it enters the country near three hundred miles from the South to the North, having the Eastern side of Maryland, and

and a small portion of Virginia on the same peninsula, to cover it from the Atlantic ocean. This bay is about eighteen miles broad for a considerable way, and seven where it is narrowest, the waters in most places being nine fathom deep. Through its whole extent it receives both on the Eastern and Western side a vast number of fine navigable rivers. Not to mention those of Maryland, from the side of Virginia it receives James River, York River, the Rappahannock, and the Potowmack.

All these great rivers, in the order they are here set down from South to North, discharge themselves with several smaller ones into the bay of Chesapeak; and they are all not only navigable themselves for very large vessels a prodigious way into the country, but have so many creeks, and receive such a number of smaller navigable rivers, as renders the communication of all parts of this country infinitely more easy than that of any country, without exception, in the world. The Potowmack is navigable for near two hundred miles, being nine miles broad at its mouth, and for a vast way not less than seven. The other three are navigable upwards of eighty, and in the windings of their several courses approach one another so nearly, that the distance between one and the other is in some parts not more than ten, sometimes not above five miles;

miles; whereas in others there is fifty miles space between each of these rivers. The planters load and unload vessels of great burden each at his own door; which, as their commodities are bulky, and of small value in proportion to their bulk, is a very fortunate circumstance, else they could never afford to send their tobacco to market low as they sell it, and charged as it is in England, with a duty of six times its original value.

The climate and soil of Virginia was undoubtedly much heightened in the first descriptions for political reasons; but after making all the necessary abatements which experience since taught us, we still find it a most excellent country. The heats in summer are excessively great, but not without the allay of refreshing sea breezes. The weather is changeable, and the changes sudden and violent. Their winter frosts come on without the least warning. After a warm day, towards the setting in of winter, so intense a cold often succeeds as to freeze over the broadest and deepest of their great rivers in one night; but these frosts, as well as their rains, are rather violent than of long continuance. They have frequent and violent thunder and lightning, but it does rarely any mischief. In general the sky is clear, and the air thin, pure and penetrating.

The soil in the low grounds of Virginia is a dark

a dark fat mould, which for many years without any manure, yields plentifully whatever is committed to it. The soil as you leave the rivers becomes light and sandy, is sooner exhausted then the low country, but is yet of a warm and generous nature, which helped by a kindly sun, yields tobacco and corn extremely well. There is no better wheat than what is produced in this province and Maryland; but the culture of tobacco employs all their attention, and almost all their hands; so that they scarcely cultivate wheat enough for their own use.

It may be judged from the climate and the soil I have described, in what excellence and plenty every sort of fruit is found in Virginia. Their forests are full of timber trees of all kinds; and their plains are covered for almost the whole year with a prodigious number of flowers, and flowering shrubs, of colours so rich, and of a scent so fragrant, that they occasioned the name of Florida to be originally given to this country. This country produces several medicinal herbs and roots, particularly the snake root; and of late the celebrated ginseng of the Chinese has been discovered there.

Horned cattle and hogs have multiplied almost beyond belief; though at the first settlement the country was utterly destitute of these animals. The meat of the former is as much below the flesh of our oxen, as that of the latter exceeds that of our hogs. The animals natural to the country are deer, of which there are great numbers; a fort of panther or tyger; bears, wolves, foxes, racoons, fquirrels, wild cats, and one very uncommon animal called the opoffum. This creature is about the fize of a cat, and befides the belly which it has in common with all others, has a falfe one beneath it, with a pretty large aperture at the end towards the hinder legs. Within this bag, or belly on the ufual parts of the common belly, are a number of teats; upon thefe, when the female of this creature conceives, the young are formed, and there they hang like fruit upon the ftalk, until they grow in bulk and weight to their appointed fize; then they drop off, and are received in the falfe belly, from which they go out at pleafure, and in which they take refuge when any danger threatens them.

They have all our forts of tame and wild fowl in equal perfection, and fome which we have not; and a vaft number of birds of various kinds, valuable for their beauty or their note. The white owl of Virginia is far larger than the fpecies which we have, and is all over of a bright filver coloured plumage, except one black fpot upon his breaft; they have the nightingale called from the country, a moft beautiful one, whofe feathers are crimfon and blue; the mocking bird, thought to excel all others in his own note, and he imitates the notes of all others; the rock bird, very sociable, and his society very agreeable by the sweetness of his music; the humming bird, the smallest of all the winged creation, and the most beautiful, all arrayed in scarlet, green and gold. This bird is said to live by licking off the dew that adheres to the flowers; he is too delicate to be brought alive into England. The sea-coasts and rivers of Virginia abound not only in several of the species of fish known in Europe, but in most of those kinds which are peculiar to America. The reptiles are many; it were tedious to enumerate all the kinds of serpents bred here; the rattle snake is the principal, and too well known in general to need any description.

CHAP. XV.

Towns in Virginia few and small. Tobacco, its cultivation. Trade in that and other commodities. People in Virginia. White and black.

THE great commodiousness of navigation, and the scarcity of handicraftsmen, have rendered all the attempts of the government to establish towns in Virginia ineffectual. James's-town, which was anciently the capital, is dwindled into an insignificant

nificant village; and Williamſburg, though the capital at preſent, the ſeat of the governor, the place of holding the aſſembly and courts of juſtice, and a college for the ſtudy of arts and ſciences, is yet but a ſmall town. However, in this town are the beſt public buildings in Britiſh America. The college one hundred and thirty-five feet long in front, reſembling Chelſea hoſpital; the capital directly facing it at the other end of the deſign of a noble ſtreet, not unlike the college in the faſhion and the ſize of the building, where the aſſembly and courts of juſtice are held, and the public offices kept; and the church, in the form of a croſs, large and well ornamented.

The great ſtaple commodity of this country, as well as Maryland, is tobacco. This plant is aboriginal in America, and of very ancient uſe, though neither ſo generally cultivated, nor ſo well manufactured as it has been ſince the coming of the Europeans. When at its juſt height, it is as tall as an ordinary ſized man; the ſtalk is ſtraight, hairy, and clammy; the leaves alternate, of a faded yellowiſh green, and towards the lower part of the plant of a great ſize. The ſeeds of tobacco are firſt ſown in beds, from whence they are tranſplanted the firſt rainy weather, into a ground diſpoſed into little hillocks like an hop garden. In a month's time from their tranſplantation they become a foot high; they then

then top them, and prune off the lower leaves, and with great attention clean them from weeds and worms twice a week; in about six weeks after, they attain to their full growth, and they begin then to turn brownish. By these marks they judge the tobacco to be ripe. They cut down the plants as faſt as they ripen, heap them up and let them lie a night to ſweat; the next day they carry them to the tobacco houſe, which is built to admit as much air as is conſiſtent with keeping out rain, where they are hung ſeparately to dry for four or five weeks, then they take them down in moiſt weather, for elſe they will crumble to duſt. After this they are laid upon ſticks, and covered up cloſe to ſweat for a week or two longer; the ſervants ſtrip and ſort them, the top being the beſt, the bottom the worſt tobacco; then they make them up in hogſheads, or form them into rolls. Wet ſeaſons muſt be carefully laid hold on for all this work, elſe the tobacco will not be ſufficiently pliable.

In trade they diſtinguiſh two ſorts of tobacco, the firſt is called Aranokoe, from Maryland and the Northern parts of Virginia; this is ſtrong and hot in the mouth, but it ſells very well in the markets of Holland, Germany, and the North. The other ſort is called ſweet ſcented, the beſt of which is from James's and York rivers in the South-

ern

ern parts of Virginia. There is no commodity to which the revenue is so much obliged as to this. It produces a vast sum, and yet appears to lay but a very inconsiderable burden upon the people in England; all the weight in reality falls upon the planter, who is kept down by the lowness of the original price; and as we have two provinces which deal in the same commodity, if the people of Virginia were to take measures to straiten the market, and raise the price, those of Maryland would certainly take the advantage of it; the people of Virginia would take the same advantage of those of Maryland in a like case. They have no prospect of ever bettering their condition; and they are the less able to endure it as they live in general luxuriously, and to the full extent of their fortunes. Therefore any failure in the sale of their goods, brings them heavily in debt to the merchants in London, who get mortgages on their estates, which are consumed to the bone, with the canker of an eight per cent usury. But however the planters may complain of the tobacco trade, the revenue flourishes by it, for it draws near three hundred thousand a year from this one article only; and the exported tobacco, the far greater part of the profits of which come to the English merchant, brings almost as great a sum annually into the kingdom. To say nothing of the great advantage we derive from being supplied from our own colonies with that for which the rest of Europe pays ready money, besides the employment of two hundred large vessels, and a proportionable number of seamen, which are occupied in this trade. From us the Virginians take every article for convenience or ornament which they use; their own manufacture does not deserve to be mentioned. The two colonies export about eighty thousand hogsheads of tobacco of eight hundred weight. They likewise trade largely with the West-Indies in lumber, pitch, tar, corn, and provisions. They send home flax, hemp, iron, staves, and walnut and cedar plank.

The number of white people in Virginia, is between sixty and seventy thousand; and they are growing every day more numerous, by the migration of the Irish, who not succeeding so well in Pensylvania, as the more frugal and industrious Germans, sell their lands in that province to the latter, and take up new ground in the remote counties in Virginia, Maryland, and North Carolina. These are chiefly presbyterians from the Northern part of Ireland, who in America are generally called Scotch Irish. In Virginia there are likewise settled a considerable number of French refugees; but much the larger part of the inhabitants are the negroe slaves, who cannot be much fewer than a hundred thousand

sand souls; they annually import into the two tobacco colonies between three and four thousand of these slaves. The negroes here do not stand in need of such vast recruits as the West-India stock; they rather increase than diminish; a blessing derived from a more moderate labour, better food, and a more healthy climate. The inhabitants of Virginia are a chearful, hospitable, and many of them a genteel though something vain and ostentatious people; they are for the greater part of the established church of England; nor until lately did they tolerate any other. Now they have some few meeting-houses of presbyterians and quakers.

CHAP. XVI.

Attempts to settle Virginia, three unsuccessful. Settled at last by lord Delawar.

THIS of Virginia is the most ancient of our colonies. Tho' strictly speaking the first attempts to settle a colony were not made in Virginia, but in that part of North Carolina which immediately borders upon it. Sir Walter Raleigh, the most extraordinary genius of his own or perhaps any other time, a penetrating statesman, an accomplished courtier, a deep scholar, a fine writer, a great soldier, and one of the ablest seamen in the world;

world; this vaft genius that pierced fo far and ran through fo many things, was of a fiery excentric kind, which led him into daring expeditions, and uncommon projects, which not being underftood by a timid prince, and envied and hated by the rivals he had in fo many ways of life, ruined him at laft. In perfon he ran infinite rifks in Guaina in fearch of gold mines: and when this country was firft difcovered, he looked through the work of an age, at one glance, and faw how advantageous it might be made to the trade of England. He was the firft man in England who had a right conception of the advantages of fettlements abroad; he was then the only perfon who had a thorough infight into trade, and who faw clearly the proper methods of promoting it. He applied to court, and got together a company, which was compofed of feveral perfons of diftinction, and feveral eminent merchants, who agreed to open a trade and fettle a colony in that part of the world, which in honour of queen Elizabeth he called Virginia.

Raleigh had too much bufinefs upon his hands at court, and found too few to fecond him in his defigns, to enable him to fupport the eftablifhment with the fpirit in which he began it. If ever any defign had an ominous beginning, and feemed to forbid any attempts for carrying it on, it was that of the firft fettlement

tlement of Virginia. Near half of the first colony was destroyed by the savages, and the rest consumed and worn down by fatigue and famine, deserted the country, and returned home in despair. The second colony was cut off, to a man, in a manner unknown; but they were supposed to be destroyed by the Indians. The third had the same dismal fate; and the fourth quarrelling amongst themselves, neglecting their agriculture to hunt for gold, and provoking the Indians by their insolent and unguarded behaviour, lost several of their people, and were returning, the poor remains of them, in a famishing and desparate condition to England, when just in the mouth of Chesapeak bay they met the lord Delawar with a squadron, loaded with provision, and every thing for their relief and defence, who persuaded them to return.

· This nobleman travelled with as much zeal and assiduity to cherish and support the froward infancy of this unpromising colony, as some have used in its better times for purposes of another kind. Regardless of his life, and inattentive to his fortune, he entered upon this long and dangerous voyage, and accepted this barren province, which had nothing of a government but its anxieties and its cares, merely for the service of his country; and he had no other reward than that retired and inward satisfaction, which a good mind

mind feels in indulging its own propensity to virtue, and the prospect of those just honours which the latest posterity will take a pleasure in bestowing upon those, who prefer the interest of posterity to their own. After he had prevailed upon the people to return, he comforted them under their misfortunes, he pointed out their causes, and uniting the tenderness of a father with the steady severity of a magistrate, he healed their divisions, and reconciled them to authority and government, by making them feel by his conduct what a blessing it could be made.

When he had settled the colony within itself, his next care was to put them upon a proper footing with regard to the Indians, whom he found very haughty and assuming on account of the late miserable state of the English; but by some well-timed and vigorous steps he humbled them, shewed he had power to chastise them, and courage to exert that power; and after having awed them into very peaceable dispositions, and settled his colony in a very growing condition, he retired home for the benefit of his health, which by his constant attention to business, and the air of an uncultivated country, had been impaired; but he left his son, with the spirit of his father, his deputy; and Sir Thomas Gates, Sir George Summers, the honourable George Piercy, Sir Ferdinand Wenman, and Mr. Newport,

Newport, for his council. These, with other persons of rank and fortune, attended him on this expedition, which gave a credit to the colony. Though there are in England many young gentlemen of fortunes, disproportioned to their rank, I fear we should not see the names of so many of them engaged in an expedition, which had no better appearance than this had at that time.

Lord Delawar did not forget the colony on his return to England; but considering himself as nearer the fountain head, thought it his duty to turn the spring of the royal favour more copiously upon the province which he superintended. For eight years together he was indefatigable in doing every thing that could tend to the peopling, the support, and the good government of this settlement, and he died in the pursuit of the same object in his voyage to Virginia, with a large supply of people, cloathing and goods.

It is one of the most necessary, and I am sure it is one of the most pleasing parts of this design, to do justice to the names of those men, who by their greatness of mind, their wisdom and their goodness, have brought into the pale of civility and religion, these rude and uncultivated parts of the globe; who could discern the rudiments of a future people, wanting only time to be unfolded, in the seed; who could perceive amidst the losses and disappoint-appointments and expences of a beginning colony, the great advantages to be derived to their country from such undertakings; and who could pursue them in spite of the malignity and narrow wisdom of the world. The ancient world had its Osyris and Erichthonius, who taught them the use of grain; their Bacchus, who instructed them in the culture of the vine; and their Orpheus and Linus, who first built towns and formed civil societies. The people of America will not fail, when time has made things venerable, and when an intermixture of fable has moulded useful truths into popular opinions, to mention with equal gratitude, and perhaps similar heightening circumstances, her Columbus, her Castro, her Gasca, her De Poincy, her Delawar, her Baltimore, and her Pen.

CHAP. XVII.

Virginia holds out against Cromwell, and is reduced. Bacon's rebellion. Its causes. Bacon dies. Peace restored.

THE colony of Virginia was so fast rooted by the care of lord Delawar, that it was enabled to stand two terrible storms; two massacres made by the Indians, in which the whole colony was nearly cut off; and to subdue that people, so as to put

it

it utterly out of their power for many years paſt to give them the leaſt diſturbance.

In the fatal troubles which brought Charles the firſt to the block, and overturned the conſtitution of England, many of the cavaliers fled for refuge to this colony, which by the general dipoſition of the inhabitants, and the virtue of Sir William Berkley, held out for the crown, until the parliament, rather by ſtratagem than force, reduced them. And what is remarkable, if it may be depended upon with any certainty, they depoſed Cromwell's governor, ſet up Sir William Berkley again, and declared for king Charles the ſecond, a good while even before the news of Oliver's death could arrive in America.

After the reſtoration, there is nothing very intereſting in their hiſtory; except that ſoon after, a ſort of rebellion aroſe in the province from miſmanagements in the government, from the decay of their trade, and from exorbitant grants inconſiderately made, which included the ſettled property of many people; theſe grievances raiſed a general diſcontent amongſt the planters, which was fomented and brought to blaze out into an actual war, by a young gentleman whoſe name was Bacon. He was an agreeable man, of a graceful preſence, and winning carriage. He had been bred to the law, had a lively and fluent expreſſion,

pression, fit to set off a popular cause, and to influence men who were ready to hear whatever could be said to colour in a proper manner what was already strongly drawn by their own feelings. This man by a specious, or perhaps a real tho' ill-judged regard for the public good, finding the governor slow in his preparations against the Indians, who were at that time ravaging the frontiers of the province, took up arms without any commission, to act against the enemy. When he had sufficient force for this purpose, he found himself in a condition not only to act against the enemy, but to give law to the governor, and to force him to give a sanction by his authority, to those proceedings which were meant to destroy it.

Bacon armed with the commission of a general, and followed by the whole force of the colony, prepared to march against the Indians; when Sir William Berkley, the governor, freed from the immediate terror of his forces, recalled him, proclaimed him a traitor, and issued a reward for apprehending him as such. This brought matters to extremities; the people were universally inflamed; Bacon adhered to what he had done, the people adhered to Bacon; and the governor, who seemed no ways inclined to temporize or yield to the storm, fled over the river Potowmack, and proclaimed all Bacon's adherents traitors. He put

put himself at the head of a small body of troops which he had raised in Maryland, and of such of the Virginians as were faithful to him, and wrote to England for supplies. On the other hand, Bacon marched to the capital, called an assembly, and for six months together disposed all things according to his own pleasure. Every thing was now hastening to a civil war, when all was quieted in as sudden a manner as it had begun, by the natural death of Bacon, in the very height of the confusion. The people unable to act without a head, proposed terms of accommodation; the terms were listened to, and peace was restored and kept without any disturbance, not so much by the removal of the grievances complained of, as by the arrival of a regiment from England, which remained a long time in the country. It must be remarked in honour of the moderation of the government, that no person suffered in his life, or his estate, for this rebellion, which was the more extraordinary as many people at that time were very earnest in solliciting grants of land in Virginia.

The events in all countries which are not the residence of the supreme power, and have no concern in the great business of transacting war and peace, have generally but little to engage the attention of the reader. I have therefore intirely omitted the tedious detail of the governors and their several transactions, with which my materials so plentifully supply me; and for the same reason I shall be very concise in my account of Maryland, which agreeing altogether with Virginia in its climate, soil, products, trade, and genius of the inhabitants, and having few or no remarkable events to recommend it, will save much trouble in that article.

CHAP. XVIII.

Maryland. The time of settling it. Grant to lord Baltimore. Attempts of king James to deprive him of his jurisdiction. He is deprived of it on the revolution. He is restored. Capital of Maryland. Its trade and inhabitants.

IT was in the reign of Charles the first, that the Lord Baltimore applied for a patent for a part of Virginia, and obtained in 1632, a grant of a tract of land upon Chesapeak bay, of about an hundred and forty miles long, and an hundred and thirty broad, having Pensylvania, then in the hands of the Dutch, upon the North, the Atlantic ocean upon the East, and the river Potowmack upon the South; in honour of the queen he called this province Maryland.

Lord Baltimore was a Roman catholic, and was induced to attempt this settlement in America,

America; in hopes of enjoying liberty of conscience for himself, and for such of his friends to whom the severity of the laws might loosen their ties to their country, and make them prefer an easy banishment with freedom, to the conveniencies of England, embittered as they were by the sharpness of the laws, and the popular odium which hung over them. The court at that time was certainly very little inclined to treat the Roman catholics in a harsh manner, neither had they in reality the least appearance of reason to do so; but the laws themselves were of a rigorous constitution; and however the court might be inclined to relax them, they could not in policy do it, but with great reserve. The puritan party perpetually accused the court, and indeed the espiscopal church, of a desire of returning to popery; and this accusation was so popular, that it was not in the power of the court to shew the papists that indulgence which they desired. The laws were still executed with very little mitigation; and they were in themselves of a much keener temper, than those which had driven the puritans about the same time to seek a refuge in the same part of the world. These reasons made lord Baltimore desirous to have, and the court willing to give him, a place of retreat in America.

The settlement of the colony cost the lord Baltimore a large sum. It was made under his auspices by his brother, and about two hundred persons, Roman catholics, and most of them of good families. This settlement at the beginning did not meet with the same difficulties, which embarrassed and retarded most of the others we had made. The people were generally of the better sort, a proper subordination was observed amongst them, and the Indians gave and took so little offence, that they ceded one half of their principal town, and some time after the whole of it to these strangers. The Indian women taught ours how to make bread of their corn; their men went out to hunt and fish with the English; they assisted them in the chace, and sold them the game they took themselves for a trifling consideration; so that the new settlers had a sort of town ready built, ground ready cleared for their subsistence, and no enemy to harrass them.

They lived thus, without much trouble or fear, until some ill-disposed persons in Virginia insinuated to the Indians, that the Baltimore colony had designs upon them; that they were Spaniards and not Englishmen, and such other stories as they judged proper to sow the seeds of suspicion and enmity in the minds of these people. Upon the first appearance,

appearance, that the malice of the Virginians had taken effect, the new planters were not wanting to themselves. They built a good fort with all expedition, and took every other necessary measure for their defence; but they continued still to treat the Indians with so much kindness, that partly by that and partly by the awe of their arms, the ill designs of their enemies were defeated.

As the colony met with so few obstructions, and as the Roman catholics in England were yet more severely treated in proportion as the court party declined, numbers constantly arrived to replenish the settlement; which the lord proprietor omitted no care, and witheld no expence to support and encourage; until the usurpation overturned the government at home, and deprived him of his rights abroad. Maryland remained under the governors appointed by the parliament and by Cromwell until the restoration, when lord Baltimore was reinstated in his former possessions, which he cultivated with his former wisdom, care and moderation. No people could live in greater ease and security; and his lordship, willing that as many as possible should enjoy the benefits of his mild and equitable administration, gave his consent to an act of assembly, which he had before promoted in his province, for allowing a free and unlimited toleration for all who professed the christian religion of whatever denomination. This liberty, which was never in the least instance violated, encouraged a great number, not only of the church of England, but of presbyterians, quakers, and all kinds of dissenters, to settle in Maryland, which, before that was almost wholly in the hands of Roman catholics.

This lord, though guilty of no maleadministration in his government, though a zealous Roman catholic, and firmly attached to the cause of king James the second, could not prevent his charter from being questioned in that arbitrary reign, and a suit from being commenced to deprive him of the property and jurisdiction of a province granted by the royal favour, and peopled at such a vast expence of his own. But it was the error of that weak and unfortunate reign, neither to know its friends, nor its enemies; but by a blind precipitate conduct to hurry on every thing of whatever consequence with almost equal heat, and to imagine that the sound of the royal authority was sufficient to justify every sort of conduct to every sort of people. But these injuries could not shake the honour and constancy of lord Baltimore, nor tempt him to desert the cause of his master. Upon the revolution he had no reason to expect any favour; yet he met with more than king James had intended him; he was deprived indeed of all his jurisdiction, but he was left
the

the profits of his province, which were by no means inconsiderable; and when his descendents had conformed to the church of England, they were restored to all their rights as fully as the legiflature has thought fit that any proprietor should enjoy them.

When upon the revolution power changed hands in that province, the new men made but an indifferent requital for the liberties and indulgences they had enjoyed under the old administration. They not only deprived the Roman catholics of all share in the government, but of all the rights of freemen; they have even adopted the whole body of the penal laws of England against them; they are at this day meditating new laws in the same spirit, and they would undoubtedly go to the greatest lengths in this respect, if the moderation and good sense of the government in England did not set some bounds to their bigotry; thinking very prudently that it were highly unjust, and equally impolitic, to allow an asylum abroad to any religious persuasions which they judged it improper to tolerate at home, and then to deprive them of its protection, recollecting at the same time in the various changes which our religion and government has undergone, which have in their turns rendered every sort of party and religion obnoxious to the reigning powers, that this American asylum which

which has been admitted in the hotteſt times of perſecution at home, has proved of infinite ſervice, not only to the preſent peace of England, but to the proſperity of its commerce, and the eſtabliſhment of its power. There are a ſort of men, who will not ſee ſo plain a truth; and they are the perſons who would appear to contend moſt warmly for liberty; but it is only a party liberty for which they contend; a liberty, which they would ſtretch out one way only to narrow it in another; they are not aſhamed of uſing the very ſame pretences for perſecuting others, that their enemies uſe for perſecuting them.

This colony, as for a long time it had with Penſylvania the honour of being unſtained with any religious perſecution, ſo neither they nor the Penſylvanians have ever until very lately been harraſſed by the calamity of any war, offenſive or defenſive, with their Indian neighbours, with whom they always lived in the moſt exemplary harmony. Indeed, in a war which the Indians made upon the colony of Virginia, by miſtake they made an incurſion into the bounds of Maryland; but they were ſoon ſenſible of their miſtake, and attoned for it. This preſent war indeed has changed every thing, and the Indians have been taught to laugh at all their ancient alliances.

Maryland,

Maryland, like Virginia, has no considerable town, and for the same reason; the number of navigable creeks and rivers. Annapolis is the seat of government. It is a small but beautifully situated town upon the river Severn.

Here is the seat of the governor, and the principal custom-house collection. The people of Maryland have the same established religion with those of Virginia, that of the church of England; but here the clergy are provided for in a much more liberal manner, and they are the most decent, and the best of the clergy in North America. They export from Maryland the same things in all respects that they do from Virginia. Their tobacco is about forty thousand hogsheads. The white inhabitants are about forty thousand; the negroes upwards of sixty thousand.

CHAP. XIX.

Attempts of the French to settle Carolina. They are beat off by the Spaniards.

IT must not be forgot, that we formerly called all the coast of North America by the name of Virginia. The province properly so called, with Maryland and the Carolinas, was known by the name of South Virginia.

By the Spaniards it was confidered as part of Florida, which country they made to extend from New Mexico to the Atlantic ocean. By them it was firft difcovered; but they treated the natives with an inhumanity, which filled them with fo violent an hatred to the Spanifh name, as rendered their fettlement there very difficult; nor did they pufh it vigoroufly, as the country fhewed no marks of producing gold or filver, the only things for which the Spaniards then valued any country. Florida therefore remained under an entire neglect in Europe, until the reign of Charles the ninth, king of France.

The celebrated leader of the proteftants in that kingdom, the admiral Chaftillon, who was not only a great commander but an able ftatefman, was a man of too comprehenfive views not to fee the advantages of a fettlement in America; he procured two veffels to be fitted out for difcoveries upon that coaft. He had it probably in his thoughts to retire thither with thofe of his perfuafion, if the fuccefs which hitherto fuited fo ill with his great courage and conduct, fhould at laft entirely deftroy his caufe in France. Thefe fhips in two months arrived upon the coaft of America; near the river now called Albemarle in the province of North Carolina. The French gave the Indians to underftand in the beft manner they were able, that they

were

were enemies to the Spaniards, which secured them a friendly reception, and the good offices of the inhabitants. They were, however, in no condition to make any settlement.

On their return to France, the admiral, at this time by the abominable policy of the court apparently in great favour, was so well satisfied with the account they had given of the country, that in 1564 he fitted out five or six ships with as many hundred men aboard, to begin a colony there. This was accordingly done at the place of their landing in the first expedition. They built a fort here, which they called Fort Charles, as they called the whole country Carolina in honour of their king then reigning. The Spaniards, who had intelligence of their proceedings, dispatched a considerable force to attack this colony, who not satisfied with reducing it, put all the people to the sword after quarter given; and committing great outrages upon the natives, they paved the way for the vengeance which soon after fell upon them for such an unnecessary and unprovoked act of cruelty. For though the admiral and his party were by this time destroyed in the infamous massacre of St. Bartholomew, and though the design of a colony died with him, one M. de Gorgues, a private gentleman, fitted out some ships, which sailed to that coast purely to revenge the murder of his countrymen, and his friends.

The Indians greedily embraced the opportunity of becoming aſſociates in the puniſhment of the common enemy. They joined in the ſiege of two or three forts the Spaniards had built there; they took them, and in all of them put the garriſon to the ſword without mercy.

Satisfied with this action the adventurers returned, and happily for us, the French court did not underſtand, blinded as they were by their bigotry, the advantages which might have been derived from giving America to the proteſtants, as we afterwards did to the diſſenters, as a place of refuge; if they had taken this ſtep, moſt certainly we ſhould have either had no ſettlements in America at all, or they muſt have been ſmall in extent, and precarious in their tenure, to what they are at this day.

CHAP. XX.

Carolina is ſettled by the Engliſh. Its conſtitution. The lords proprietors reſign their charter. Made a royal government, and divided into two provinces.

AFTER the French expedition, the country of Carolina remained without any attention from Spaniards, French or Engliſh, until, as we obſerved in the article of Virginia, Sir Walter Raleigh projected an
eſtabliſh-

establishment there. It was not in the part now called Virginia, but in North Carolina, that our first unhappy settlements were made and destroyed. Afterwards the adventurers entered the bay of Chesapeak, and fixed a permanent colony to the Northward; so that although Carolina was the first part of the Atlantic coast of America, which had an European colony, yet by an odd caprice it was for a long time deserted by both England and France, who settled with infinitely more difficulty in climates much less advantageous or agreeable.

It was not until the year 1663, in the reign of Charles the second, that we had any notion of formally settling that country. In that year the earl of Clarendon lord Chancellor, the duke of Albemarle, the lord Craven, lord Berkley, lord Ashley, afterwards earl of Shaftesbury, Sir George Carteret, Sir William Berkley, and Sir George Colleton, obtained a charter for the property and jurisdiction of that country, from the 31st degree of North latitude to the 36th; and being invested with full power to settle and govern the country, they had the model of a constitution framed, and a body of fundamental laws compiled by the famous philosopher Mr. Locke. On this plan the lords proprietors themselves stood in the place of the king, gave their assent or dissent as they thought proper to all laws, appointed

pointed all officers, and bestowed all titles of dignity. In his turn one of these lords acted for the rest. In the province they appointed two other branches, in a good measure analogous to the legislature in England. They made three ranks, or rather classes of nobility. The lowest was composed of those to whom they had made grants of twelve thousand acres of land, whom they called barons; the next order had twenty-four thousand acres, or two baronies, with the title of cassiques; these were to answer our earls; the third had two cassiqueships, or forty-eight thousand acres, and were called landgraves, a title in that province analogous to duke. This body formed the upper house; their lands were not alienable by parcels. The lower house was formed, as it is in the other colonies, of representatives from the several towns or counties. But the whole was not called, as in the rest of the plantations, an assembly, but a parliament.

They began their first settlement at a point of land towards the Southward of their district, between two navigable rivers, though of no long course, called Ashley and Cowper rivers, and there laid the foundation of a city, called Charles-town, which was designed to be, what it now is, the capital of the province. They expended about twelve thousand pounds in the first settlement. But it was not chiefly

to

to the funds of the lords proprietors, that this province owed its eftablifhment. They obferved what advantages the other colonies derived from opening an harbour for refugees; and not only from this confideration, but from the humane difpofition of that excellent man who formed the model of their government, they gave an unlimitted toleration to people of all religious perfuafions. This induced a great number of diffenters, over whom the then government held a more fevere hand than was confiftent with juftice or policy, to tranfport themfelves with their fortunes and families into Carolina. They became foon at leaft as numerous as the churchmen; and though they difplayed none of that frantic bigotry which difgraced the New England refugees, they could not preferve themfelves from the jealoufy and hatred of thofe of the church of England, who having a majority in one of the affemblies, attempted to exclude all diffenters from a right of fitting there. This produced diffentions, tumults, and riots every day, which tore the colony to pieces, and hindered it for many years from making that progrefs which might be expected from its great natural advantages. The people fell into difputes of no lefs violent a nature with the lords proprietors, and provoking the Indians by a feries of unjuft and violent actions, they gave occafion to two wars, in which however

ever they were victorious, and subdued almost all the Indian nations within their own bounds at this side of the Apalachian mountains.

Their intestine distractions, and their foreign wars, kept the colony so low, that an act of parliament, if possible to prevent the last ruinous consequences of these divisions, put the province under the immediate care and inspection of the crown. The lords proprietors making a virtue of necessity, accepted a recompence of about twenty-four thousand pounds, both for the property and jurisdiction; except the earl Granville, who kept his eighth part of the property, which comprehends very near half of North Carolina, on that part which immediately borders upon the province of Virginia. Their constitution in those points wherein it differed from that of the other colonies, was altered; and the country, for the more commodious administration of affairs, was divided into two distinct independent governments, called North Carolina and South Carolina. This was in the year 1728. In a little time a firm peace was established with all the neighbouring Indian nations, the Cherokees, the Creeks, and the Cataubas; the province began to breathe from its internal quarrels; and its trade has advanced every year since that time with an astonishing rapidity.

CHAP.

CHAP. XXI.

Situation, climate, &c. of Carolina. Its animal and vegetable productions.

THESE two provinces lying between the 31ſt and 36th degrees of latitude, are upwards of four hundred miles in length, and in breadth to the Indian nations, near three hundred. The climate and ſoil in theſe countries, do not conſiderably differ from thoſe of Virginia; but where they differ, it is much to the advantage of Carolina, which on the whole may be conſidered one of the fineſt climates in the world. The heat in ſummer is very little greater than in Virginia; but the winters are milder and ſhorter, and the year in all reſpects does not come to the ſame violent extremities. However the weather, though in general ſerene as the air is healthy, yet like all American weather, it makes ſuch quick changes, and thoſe ſo ſharp, as to oblige the inhabitants to rather more caution in their dreſs and diet, than we are obliged to uſe in Enrope. Thunder and lightning is frequent; and it is the only one of our colonies upon the continent which is ſubject to hurricanes; but they are very rare, and not near ſo violent as thoſe of the Weſt-Indies. Part of the month of March, and all April, May, and the greatest part of June, are here inexpressibly temperate and agreeable, but in July, August, and for almost the whole of September, the heat is very intense; and though the winters are sharp, especially when the North-West wind prevails, yet they are seldom severe enough to freeze any considerable water; effecting only the mornings and evenings, the frosts have never sufficient strength to resist the noon-day sun; so that many tender plants which do not stand the winter of Virginia, flourish in Carolina; for they have oranges in great plenty near Charles-town, and excellent in their kinds, both sweet and sour. Olives are rather neglected by the planter, than denied by the climate. The vegetation of every kind of plant is here almost incredibly quick; for there is something so kindly in the air and soil, that where the latter has the most barren and unpromising appearance, if neglected for a while, of itself it shoots out an immense quantity of those various plants and beautiful flowering shrubs and flowers, for which this country is so famous, and of which Mr. Catesby in his Natural History of Carolina has made such fine drawings.

The whole country is in a manner one forest, where our planters have not cleared it. The trees are almost the same in every respect with those produced in Virginia; and by the different species of these, the quality of the

soil

soil is easily known; for those grounds which bear the oak, the walnut, and the hickory, are extremely fertile; they are of a dark sand, intermixed with loam, and as all their land abounds with nitre, it is a long time before it is exhausted; for here they never use any manure. The pine barren is the worst of all; this is an almost perfectly white sand, yet it bears the pine tree and some other useful plants naturally, yielding good profit in pitch, tar, and turpentine; when this species of land is cleared, for two or three years together it produces very tolerable crops of Indian corn and pease; and when it lies low and is flooded, it even answers well for rice. But what is the best of all for this province, this worst species of its land is favourable to a species of the most valuable of all its products, to one of the kinds of indigo. There is another sort of ground, which lies low and wet upon the banks of some of their rivers; this is called swamp, which in some places is in a manner useless, in others it is far the richest of all their grounds; it is a black fat earth, and bears their great staple rice, which must have in general a rich moist soil, in the greatest plenty and perfection. The country near the sea and at the mouths of the navigable rivers, is much the worst; for the most of the land there is of the species of the pale, light, sandy-coloured ground; and what is otherwise in those parts, is little better than an unhealthy and unprofitable salt marsh; but the country, as you advance in it, improves continually; and at an hundred miles distance from Charlestown, where it begins to grow hilly, the soil is of a prodigious fertility, fitted for every purpose of human life. The air is pure and wholsome, and the summer heats much more temperate than in the flat country; for Carolina is all an even plain for eighty miles from the sea; no hill, no rock, scarce even a pebble to be met with: so that the best part of the maritime country, from this sameness, must want something of the fine effect which its beautiful products would have by a more variegated and advantageous disposition; but nothing can be imagined more pleasant to the eye than the back country, and its fruitfulness is almost incredible. Wheat grows extremely well there, and yields a prodigious increase. In the other parts of Carolina they raise but little, where it is apt to mildew and spend itself in straw; and these evils the planters take very little care to redress, as they turn their whole attention to the culture of rice, which is more profitable, and in which they are unrivalled; being supplied with what wheat they want in exchange for this grain, from New York and Pensylvania.

The land in Carolina is very easily cleared every where, as there is little or no underwood.

wood. Their forests consist mostly of great trees at a considerable distance asunder; so that they can clear in Carolina more land in a week, than in the forests of Europe they can do in a month. Their method is to cut them at about a foot from the ground, and then saw the trees into boards, or convert them into staves, heading, or other species of lumber, according to the nature of the wood, or the demands at the market. If they are too far from navigation, they heap them together, and leave them to rot. The roots soon decay; and before that they find no inconvenience from them, where land is so plenty.

The aboriginal animals of this country are in general the same with those of Virginia, but there is yet a greater number and variety of beautiful fowls. All the animals of Europe are here in plenty; black cattle are multiplied prodigiously. About fifty years ago, it was a thing extraordinary to have above three or four cows, now some have a thousand; some in North Carolina a great many more; but to have two or three hundred is very common. These ramble all day at pleasure in the forests; but their calves being separated, and kept in fenced pastures, the cows return every evening to them; they are then milked, detained all night, milked in the morning, and then let loose again. The hogs range in the same manner, and return like the cows, by having shelter and some victuals provided for them at the plantation; these are vastly numerous, and many quite wild; many horned cattle and horses too run wild in their woods; though at their first settlement there was not one of these animals in the country. They drive a great many cattle from North Carolina every year into Virginia, to be slaughtered there; and they kill and salt some beef, and a good deal of pork, for the West-Indies, within themselves; but the beef is neither so good, nor does it keep near so long as what is sent to the same market from Ireland. They export a considerable number of live cattle to Pensylvania and the West-Indies. Sheep are not so plenty as the black cattle or hogs, neither is their flesh so good; their wooll is very ordinary.

CHAP. XXII.

The commodities of Carolina for export. Rice, indigo, pitch and tar. Process in raising and manufacturing these commodities.

THE trade of Carolina, besides the lumber, provision, and the like, which it yields in common with the rest of America, has three great staple commodities, indigo, rice, and the produce of the pine, turpentine, tar, and pitch, The two former commodities

modities South Carolina has intirely to itself; and taking in North Carolina, this part of America yields more pitch and tar than all the rest of our colonies.

Rice anciently formed by itself the staple of this province; this wholsome grain makes a great part of the food of all ranks of people in the Southern parts of the world; in the Northern it is not so much in request. Whilst the rigour of the act of navigation obliged them to send all their rice directly to England, to be re-shipped for the markets of Spain and Portugal; the charges incident to this regulation lay so heavy upon the trade, that the cultivation of rice, especially in time of war, when these charges were greatly aggravated by the rise of the freight and insurance, hardly answered the charges of the planter; but now the legislature has relaxed the law in this respect, and permits the Carolinians to send their rice directly to any place to the Southward of Cape Finisterre. This prudent indulgence has again revived the rice trade; and though they have gone largely, and with great spirit into the profitable article of indigo, it has not diverted their attention from the cultivation of rice; they raise now above double the quantity of what they raised some years ago; and this branch alone of their commerce is, at the lowest estimation, worth one hundred and fifty thousand pounds sterling annually.

Indigo is a dye made from a plant of the same name, which probably was so called from India, where it was first cultivated, and from whence we had for a considerable time the whole of what we consumed in Europe. This plant is very like the fern when grown, and when young hardly distinguishable from lucern-grass; its leaves in general are pennated, and terminated by a single lobe; the flowers consist of five leaves, and are of the papilionaceous kind, the uppermost petal being larger and rounder than the rest, and lightly furrowed on the side; the lower ones are short and end in a point; in the middle of the flower is situated the stile, which afterwards becomes a pod, containing the seeds.

They cultivate three sorts of indigo in Carolina, which demand the same variety of soils. First, the French or Hispaniola indigo, which striking a long tap-root, will only flourish in a deep rich soil; and therefore, though an excellent sort, it is not so much cultivated in the maritime parts of Carolina, which are generally sandy; but no part of the world is more fit to produce it in perfection than the same country, an hundred miles backwards; it is neglected too on another account, for it hardly bears a winter so sharp as that of Carolina.

The second sort, which is the false guatemala, or true bahama, bears the winter better, is a more tall and vigorous plant, is raised in greater quantities from the same compass of ground; is content with the worst soils in the country, and is therefore more cultivated than the first sort, though inferior in the quality of its dye.

The third sort is the wild indigo, which is indigenous here; this, as it is a native of the country, answers the purposes of the planter the best of all, with regard to the hardiness of the plant, the easiness of the culture, and the quantity of the produce; of the quality there is some dispute, not yet settled amongst the planters themselves; nor can they as yet distinctly tell when they are to attribute the faults of their indigo to the nature of the plant, to the seasons, which have much influence upon it, or to some defect in the manufacture.

The time of planting the indigo, is generally after the first rains succeeding the vernal equinox; the seed is sowed in small straight trenches, about eighteen or twenty inches asunder; when it is at its height, it is generally eighteen inches tall. It is fit for cutting, if all things answer well, in the beginning of July. Towards the end of August a second cutting is obtained; and if they have a mild autumn, there is a third cutting at Michaelmas; the indigo land must be weeded every day, and the plants cleansed from worms, and
the

the plantation attended with the greatest care and diligence; about twenty-five negroes may manage a plantation of fifty acres, and compleat the manufacture of the drug, besides providing their own necessary subsistence, and that of the planter's family. Each acre yields, if the land be very good, sixty or seventy pounds weight of indigo; at a medium the produce is fifty pounds. When the plant is beginning to blossom it is fit for cutting; and when cut, great care ought to be taken to bring it to the steeper, without pressing or shaking it, as a great part of the beauty of the indigo depends upon the fine farina which adheres to the leaves of this plant.

The apparatus for making indigo is pretty considerable, though not very expensive; for besides a pump, the whole consists only of vats and tubs of cypress wood, common and cheap in this country. The indigo when cut is first laid in a vat about twelve or fourteen foot long, and four deep, to the height of about fourteen inches, to macerate and digest. Then this vessel, which is called the steeper, is filled with water; the whole having lain from about twelve or sixteen hours, according to the weather, begins to ferment, swell, rise, and grow sensibly warm; at this time spars of wood are run across to prevent its rising too much, and a pin is then set to mark the highest point of its ascent; when it falls below

low this mark they judge that the fermentation has attained its due pitch, and begins to abate; this directs the manager to open a cock, and let off the water into another vat, which is called the beater; the grofs matter that remains in the firft vat, is carried off to manure the ground, for which purpofe it is excellent, and new cuttings are put in as long as the harveft of this weed continues.

When the water, ftrongly impregnated with the particles of the Indigo, has run into the fecond vat or beater, they attend with a fort of bottomlefs buckets, with long handles, to work and agitate it; which they do inceffantly until it heats, froths, ferments, and rifes above the rim of the veffel which contains it; to allay this violent fermentation, oil is thrown in as the froth rifes, which inftantly finks it. When this beating has continued for twenty, thirty, or thirty-five minutes, according to the ftate of the weather, (for in cool weather it requires the longeft continued beating) a fmall muddy grain begins to be formed, the falts and other particles of the plant united and diffolved before with the water, are now reunited, and begin to granulate.

To difcover thefe particles the better, and to find when the liquor is fufficiently beaten, they take up fome of it from time to time on a plate or in a glafs; when it appears in an hopeful condition, they let loofe fome lime water

water from an adjacent veſſel, gently ſtirring the whole, which wonderfully facilitates the operation; the indigo granulates more fully, the liquor aſſumes a purpliſh colour, and the whole is troubled and muddy; it is now ſuffered to ſettle; then the clearer part is let to run off into another ſucceſſion of veſſels, from whence the water is conveyed away as faſt as it clears at the top, until nothing remains but a thick mud, which is put into bags of coarſe linen. Theſe are hung up and left for ſome time until the moiſture is entirely drained off. To finiſh the drying this mud is turned out of the bags, and worked upon boards of ſome porous timber with a wooden ſpatula; it is frequently expoſed to the morning and evening ſun, but for a ſhort time only; and then it is put into boxes or frames, which is called the curing, expoſed again to the ſun in the ſame cautious manner, until with great labour and attention the operation is finiſhed, and that valuable drug called indigo, fitted for the market. The greateſt ſkill and care is required in every part of the proceſs, or there may be great danger of ruining the whole; the water muſt not be ſuffered to remain too ſhort or too long a time, either in the ſteeper or beater; the beating itſelf muſt be nicely managed ſo as not to exceed or fall ſhort; and in the curing, the exact medium between too much or too little drying is not eaſily attained.

tained. Nothing but experience can make the overseer skilful in these matters.

There are two methods of trying the goodness of indigo; by fire and by water; if it swims it is good, if it sinks it is naught, the heavier the worse; so if it wholly dissolves in water it is good. Another way of proving is, by the fire ordeal; if it entirely burns away it is good, the adulterations remain untouched.

There is perhaps no branch of manufacture, in which so large profits may be made upon so moderate a fund, as that of indigo; and there is no country in which this manufacture can be carried on to such advantage as in Carolina, where the climate is healthy, provision plentiful and cheap, and every thing necessary for that business had with the greatest ease. To do justice to the Carolinians, they have not neglected these advantages; and if they continue to improve them with the same spirit in which they have begun, and attend diligently to the quality of their goods, they must naturally and necessarily come to supply the whole consumption of the world with this commodity; and consequently make their country the richest, as it is the pleasantest and most fertile part of the British dominions.

In all parts of Carolina, but especially in North Carolina, they make great quantities of turpentine, tar and pitch. They are all the produce

produce of the pine. The turpentine is drawn simply from incisions made in the tree; they are made from as great an height as a man can reach with an hatchet; these incisions meet at the bottom of the tree in a point, where they pour their contents into a vessel placed to receive them. There is nothing further in this process. But tar requires a more considerable apparatus and great trouble. They prepare a circular floor of clay, declining a little towards the center; from this is laid a pipe of wood, the upper part of which is even with the floor, and reaches ten feet without the circumference; under the end the earth is dug away, and barrels placed to receive the tar as it runs. Upon the floor is built up a large pile of pine wood split in pieces, and surrounded with a wall of earth, leaving only a small aperture at the top where the fire is first kindled. When the fire begins to burn, they cover this opening likewise to confine the fire from flaming out, and to leave only sufficient heat to force the tar downwards to the floor. They temper the heat as they please, by running a stick into the wall of clay, and giving it air. Pitch is made by boiling tar in large iron kettles set in furnaces, or burning it in round clay holes made in the earth. The greatest quantity of pitch and tar is made in North Carolina.

CHAP.

CHAP. XXIII.

North Carolina, some account of its settlement. Bad state of that province. Is considerably improved. Chief town.

THERE are in the two provinces which compose Carolina, ten navigable rivers of a very long course, and innumerable smaller ones, which fall into them, all abounding in fish. About fifty or sixty miles from the sea, there are falls in most of the great rivers, which as you approach their sources, become more frequent. This is the case of almost all the American rivers; at these falls, those who navigate these rivers land their goods, carry them beyond the cataract on horses or waggons, and then re-ship them below or above it.

The mouths of the rivers in North Carolina form but ordinary harbours, and do not admit, except one at Cape Fear, vessels of above seventy or eighty tons; so that larger ships are obliged to lye off in a sound called Ocacock, which is formed between some islands and the continent. This lays a weight upon their trade by the expence of lighterage. North Carolina, partly upon that occasion, but principally that the first settlements were made as near as possible to the capital, which lies

considerably

considerably to the Southward, was greatly neglected. For a long time it was but ill inhabited, and by an indigent and disorderly people, who had little property, and hardly any law or government to protect them in what they had. As commodious land grew scarce in the other colonies, people in low circumstances observing that a great deal of excellent and convenient land was yet to be patented in North Carolina, were induced by that circumstance to plant themselves there. Others who saw how they prospered, followed their example. The government became more attentive to the place as it became more valuable; by degrees something of a better order was introduced. The effect of which is, that though by no means as wealthy as South Carolina, North Carolina has many more white people; things begin to wear a face of settlement; and the difficulties they have lain under are not so many nor so great as to make us neglect all future efforts, or hinder us from forming very reasonable expectations of seeing the trade of this country, with proper management, become a flourishing and fruitful branch of the British American commerce. That even now it is far from contemptible, may appear by a list of their exported commodities, which I shall subjoin.

Edenton was formerly the capital of North Carolina, if a trifling village can deserve that deno-

denomination; but the present governor Mr. Dobbs has projected one further South upon the river Neus; which, though it has the advantage of being something more central, is by no means equally well situated for trade, which ought always to be of the first consideration in whatever regards any of the colonies. However, none of their towns are worth mentioning; the conveniency of inland navigation in all our Southern colonies, and the want of handicraftsmen, is a great and almost insuperable obstacle to their ever having any considerable.

CHAP. XXIV.

An account of Charles-town. Port-Royal. The trade of Carolina. Its vast increase. Articles not sufficiently attended to there.

THE only town in either of the Carolinas which can draw our attention is Charles-town; and this is one of the first in North America for size, beauty, and traffic. Its situation I have already mentioned, so admirably chosen at the confluence of two navigable rivers. Its harbour is good in every respect, but that of a bar, which hinders vessels of more than two hundred tons burden from entering. The town is regularly and pretty strongly fortified both by nature and art; the streets are well cut; the houses are large and well built, and rent extremely high. The church is spacious, and executed in a very handsome taste, exceeding every thing of that kind which we have in America. Here besides the several denominations of dissenters have their meeting houses. It contains about eight hundred houses, and is the seat of the governor and the place of meeting of the assembly. Several handsome equipages are kept here. The planters and merchants are rich, and well bred; the people are showy and expensive in their dress and way of living; so that every thing conspires to make this by much the liveliest and politest place, as it is one of the richest too in all America.

The best harbour in this province is far to the Southward, on the borders of Georgia, called Port-Royal. This might give a capacious and safe reception to the largest fleets of the greatest bulk and burden; yet the town, which is called Beaufort, built upon an island of the same name with the harbour, is not as yet considerable, but it bids fair in time for becoming the first trading town in this part of America.

The import trade of South Carolina from Great Britain and the West-Indies, is the same in all respects with that of the rest of the colonies, and it is very large. Their trade with the Indians is likewise in a very flourishing

ing condition. As for its export, both the nature of that, and its prodigious increase, may be discerned from the following comparative tables, which let us see how much this colony has really advanced in a few years; as an attentive consideration of its natural advantages must shew us how much it must advance, if properly managed, as there is scarce any improvement of which this excellent country is not capable.

Exported from Charles-town,

In the year 1731.	In the year 1754.
Rice, 41,957 barrels	Rice, 104,682 barrels
Indigo, 00,000 pounds	Indigo, 216,924 pds.
Deerskins, 300 hds.	Deer skins, 460 hogsheads
Pitch, 10,750 barrels	114 bund.
Tar, 2,063 ditto	508 loose
Turpent. 759 ditto	Pitch, 5,869 barrels
Beef, pork, &c. not particularized.	Tar, 2,945 ditto
	Turpent. 759 ditto
	Beef, 416 ditto
	Pork, 1,560 ditto
	Ind. corn, 16,428 bush.
	Peas, 9,162 ditto
	Taned lea. 4,196 hides
	Hides in the hair 1,200
	Shing: 1,114,000
	Staves, 206,000
	Lumb. 395,000 feet

Besides

Besides a great deal of live cattle, horses, cedar, cypress, and walnut plank; bees wax, myrtle, and some raw silk and cotton.

North Carolina, which is reputed one of the least flourishing of our settlements, and which certainly lay under great difficulties, yet is within a few years greatly improved. The consequence of this inferior province may appear by the following view of its trade, which I can take upon me to say is not very far from being exact; it is at least sufficiently so to enable us to form a proper idea of this province, and its commerce.

Exported from all the ports of North Carolina in 1753.

Tar, 61,528 barrels.
Pitch, 12,055 ditto.
Turpentine, 10,429 ditto.
Staves, 762,330 no.
Shingles, 2,500,000 no.
Lumber, 2,000,647 feet.
Corn, 61,580 bushels.
Peas, about 10,000 ditto.
Pork & Beef, 3,300 barrels.
Tobacco, about 100 hogsheads.
Tanned lea. about 1000 hundred weight.
Deer skins in all ways, about 30,000.

Besides a very considerable quantity of wheat, rice, bread, potatoes, bees-wax, tallow, candles, bacon, hog's lard, some cotton, and a vast

vast deal of squared timber of walnut and cedar, and hoops and headings of all sorts. Of late they raise indigo, but in what quantity I cannot determine, for it is all exported from South Carolina. They raise likewise much more tobacco than I have mentioned, but this, as it is produced on the frontiers of Virginia, so it is exported from thence. They export too no inconsiderable quantity of beaver, racoon, otter, fox, minx, and wild cats, skins, and in every ship a good deal of live cattle, besides what they vend in Virginia. Both in North and South Carolina they have made frequent, but I think not vigorous nor sufficiently continued efforts in the cultivation of cotton and silk. What they have sent home of these commodities is of so excellent a kind, as to give us great encouragement to proceed in a business which we have not taken to heart with all that warmth that its importance in trade, and the fitness of the climate for these most valuable articles certainly deserves. It was a long time before this province went into the profitable trade of indigo, notwithstanding a premium subsisted a good many years for all that should be raised in our plantations; the thing was at first despaired of, and it was never judged that Carolina could produce this drug; but no sooner had a few shewn a spirited and successful example, than all went into it so heartily,

that though it is but about six years since they began, I am informed that five hundred thousand weight was made last year; and as they go on, in a very little time they will supply the market with a commodity, which before we purchased every ounce from the French and Spaniards. Silk requires still more trouble, and a closer attention; as yet it proceeds with languor, nor will a premium alone ever suffice to set on foot in a vigorous manner a manufacture which will find great difficulties in any country, which does not abound in hands that can work for very trifling wages. The want of this advantage in Carolina, though no part of the world is fitter for this business, and no business could be so advantageous to England, will for a very long time be an impediment to the manufacture of raw silk, unless some proper, well studied, and vigorously executed scheme be set on foot for that purpose; and surely it is a matter worthy of a very serious consideration. America is our great resource; this will remain to us when other branches of our trade are decayed, or exist no more; and therefore we ought to grudge no expence that may enable them to answer this end so effectually, as one day to supply the many losses we have already had, and the many more we have but too much reason to apprehend in our commerce. These expences are not like the expences of war, heavy in
their

their nature, and precarious in their effects; but when judiciously ordered, the certain and infallible means of rich and succeffive harvests of gain to the lateft pofterity, at the momentary charge of a comparatively fmall quantity of feed, and of a moderate hufbandry to the prefent generation.

CHAP. XXV.

Settlement of Georgia. Reafons for it. The plan of the fettlement defective. Attempts to remedy it.

IN the year 1732, the government obferving that a great tract of land in Carolina upon the borders of the Spanifh Florida lay wafte and unfettled, refolved to erect it into a feparate province, and to fend a colony thither. This they were the rather induced to do, becaufe it lay on the frontier of all our provinces naked and defencelefs; whereas if it could be properly fettled, it would be a ftrong barrier to them upon that fide, or at leaft would be fufficient to protect Carolina from the incurfions which the Indians, inftigated by the French or Spaniards, might make upon that province. They had it likewife in their view to raife wine, oil, and filk, and to turn the induftry of this new people from the

tim-

timber and provision trade, which the other colonies had gone into too largely, into channels more advantageous to the public. Laudable designs in every respect; though perhaps the means which were taken to put them in execution, were not altogether answerable.

That whole country which lies between the rivers Savannah and Alatamaha North and South, and from the Atlantic ocean on the East, to the great South-Sea upon the West, was vested in trustees; at the end of that period the property in chief was to revert to the crown. This country extends about sixty miles from North and South near the sea, but widens in the more remote parts to above one hundred and fifty. From the Sea to the Apalachian mountains it is not much short of three hundred.

In pursuance of the original design, the trustees resolved to encourage poor people to settle in the province, which had been committed to their care; and to this purpose found them in necessaries to transport them into a country, of which they had previously published a most exaggerated and flattering description. In reality the country differs little from South Carolina, but that the summers are yet hotter, and the soil in the general of a poorer kind. The colony was sent over under the care of Mr. Oglethorpe, who

very

very generously bestowed his own time and pains, without any reward, for the advancement of the settlement.

The trustees had very well observed, that many of our colonies, especially that of South Carolina, had been very much endangered both internally and externally, by suffering the negroes to grow so much more numerous than the whites. An error of this kind, they judged, in a colony which was not only to defend itself, but to be in some sort a protection to the others, would have been inexcusable; they for that reason forbid the importation of negroes into Georgia. In the next place, they observed that great mischiefs happened in the other settlements from making vast grants of land, which the grantees jobbed out again to the discouragement of the settlers; or what was worse, suffered to lie idle and uncultivated. To avoid this mischief, and to prevent the people from becoming wealthy and luxurious, which they thought inconsistent with the military plan upon which this colony was founded, they allowed in the common course of each family but twenty-five acres; and none could according to the original scheme, by any means come to possess more than five hundred. Neither did they give an inheritance in fee simple, or to the heirs general of the settlers, but granted them their lands inheritable only by their male issue.

iffue. They likewife forbid the importation of rum into the province, to prevent the great diforders which they obferved to arife in the other parts of North America, from the abufe of fpirituous liquors.

These regulations, though well intended, and meant to bring about very excellent purpofes, yet it might at firft, as it did afterwards appear, that they were made without fufficiently confulting the nature of the country, or the difpofition of the people which they regarded. For in the firft place, as the climate is exceffively hot, and field work very laborious in a new colony, as the ground muft be cleared, tilled and fowed, all with great and inceffant toil, for their bare fubfiftence, the load was too heavy for the white men, efpecially men who had not been feafoned to the country. The confequence of which was, that the greateft part of their time, all the heat of the day, was fpent in idlenefs, which brought certain want along with it. It is true that all our colonies on the continent, even Virginia and Carolina, were originally fettled without the help of negroes. The white men were obliged to the labour, and they underwent it, becaufe they then faw no other way; but it is the nature of man, not to fubmit to extraordinary hardfhips, in one fpot, when they fee their neighbours on another, without any difference in the circumftances

stances of things, in a much more easy condition. Besides, there were no methods taken to animate them under the hardships they endured. All things contributed to dispirit them.

A levelling scheme in a new colony is a thing extremely unadviseable. Men are seldom induced to leave their country, but upon some extraordinary prospects; there ought always to be something of a vastness in the view that is presented to them, to strike powerfully upon their imagination; and this will operate, because men will never reason well enough to see, that the majority of mankind are not endued with dispositions proper to make a fortune any where, let the proposed advantages be what they will. The majority of mankind must always be indigent; but in a new settlement they must be all so, unless some persons there are on such a comfortable and substantial footing, as to give direction and vigour to the industry of the rest; for in every well contrived building there must be strong beams and joists, as well as smaller bricks, tiles and laths. Persons of substance found themselves discouraged from attempting a settlement, by the narrow bounds which no industry could enable them to pass; and the design of confirming the inheritance to the male line was an additional discouragement. The settlers found themselves not upon a par with the other colonies. There was an obvious inconvenience in leaving no provision at all for females, as in a new colony the land muft be, for fome time at leaft, the only wealth of the family. The quantity of twenty-five acres was undoubtedly too fmall a portion, as it was given without any confideration of the quality of the land, and was therefore in many places of very little value. Add to this, that it was clogged after a fhort free tenure, with a much greater quit-rent than is paid in our beft and longeft fettled colonies. Indeed through the whole manner of granting land, there appeared, I know not what low attention to the trifling profits that might be derived to the truftees or the crown by rents and efcheats, which clogged the liberal fcheme that was firft laid down, and was in itfelf extremely injudicious. When you have a flourifhing colony, with extenfive fettlements, from the fmalleft quit-rents the crown receives a large revenue; but in an ill-fettled province, the greateft rents make but a poor return, and yet are fufficient to burden and impoverifh the people.

 The tail male grants were fo grievous, that the truftees themfelves corrected that error in a fhort time. The prohibition of rum, though fpecious in appearance, had a very bad effect. The waters in this unfettled country running through fuch an extent of foreft, were not

wholfome

wholsome drinking, and wanted the corrective of a little spirit, as the settlers themselves wanted something to support their strength in the extraordinary and unusual heat of the climate, and the dampness of it in several places disposing them to agues and fevers. But what was worse, this prohibition in a manner deprived them of the only vent they had for the only commodities they could send to market, lumber and corn, which could sell no where but in the sugar islands, and with this restriction of negroes and rum, they could take very little from them in return.

CHAP. XXVI.

Colony new modelled. Faults in the new constitution. Trade of this province.

ALL these, and several other inconveniencies in the plan of the settlement, raised a general discontent in the inhabitants; they quarrelled with one another, and with their magistrates; they complained; they remonstrated; and finding no satisfaction, many of them fled out of Georgia, and dispersed themselves where they deemed the encouragement better, to all the other colonies. So that of above two thousand people, who had transported themselves from Europe, in a little time not above six or seven hundred were to be be found in Georgia; so far were they from increasing. The mischief grew worse and worse every day, until the government revoked the grant to the trustees, took the province into their own hands, and annulled all the particular regulations that were made. It was then left exactly on the same footing with Carolina.

Though this step has probably saved the colony from entire ruin, yet it was not perhaps so well done to neglect entirely the first views upon which it was settled. These were undoubtedly judicious; and if the methods taken to compass them were not so well directed, it was no argument against the designs themselves, but a reason for some change in the instruments designed to put them in execution. Certainly nothing wants a regulation more, than the dangerous inequality in the number of negroes and whites in such of our provinces where the former are used. South Carolina, in spite of its great wealth, is really in a more defenceless condition, than a knot of poor townships on the frontiers of New England. In Georgia, the first error of absolutely prohibiting the use of negroes, might be turned to very good account; for they would have received the permission to employ them under what qualifications soever, not as a restriction, but as a favour and indulgence; and by executing whatever regulations we should make in

this

this point with strictness, by degrees we might see a province fit to answer all the ends of defence and traffic too; whereas we have let them use such a latitude in that affair, which we were so earnest to prevent, that Georgia instead of being any defence to Carolina, does actually stand in need of a considerable force to defend itself.

As for the scheme of vines and silk, we were extremely eager in this respect in the beginning; and very supine ever since. At that time such a design was clearly impracticable; because a few people seated in a wild country must first provide every thing for the support of life, by raising of corn and breeding of cattle, before they can think of manufactures of any kind; and they must grow numerous enough to spare a number of hands from that most necessary employment, before they can send such things in any degree of cheapness or plenty to a good market. But now there is little said of either of these articles, though the province is longer settled and grown more populous. But the misfortune is, that though no people upon earth originally conceive things better than the English do, they want the unremitting perseverance which is necessary to bring designs of consequence to perfection. We are apt suddenly to change our measures upon any failure; without sufficiently considering whether the failure

failure has been owing to a fault in the scheme itself; this does not arise from any defect peculiar to our people, for it is the fault of mankind in general, if left to themselves. What is done by us is generally done by the spirit of the people; as far as that can go we advance, but no farther. We want political regulations, and a steady plan in government, to remedy the defects that must be in all things, which depend merely on the character and disposition of the people.

At present Georgia is beginning to emerge, though slowly, out of the difficulties that attended its first establishment. It is still but indifferently peopled, though it is now twenty-six years since its first settlement. Not one of our colonies was of so slow a growth, though none had so much of the attention of the government, or of the people in general, or raised so great expectations in the beginning. They export some corn and lumber to the West-Indies; they raise some rice, and of late are going with success into indigo. It is not to be doubted but in time, when their internal divisions are a little better composed, the remaining errors in the government corrected, and the people begin to multiply, that they will become a useful province.

Georgia has two towns already known in trade; Savannah the capital, which stands very well for business about ten miles form the sea,

upon

upon a noble river of the same name, which is navigable two hundred miles further for large boats, to the second town, called Augusta; this stands upon a spot of ground of the greatest fertility, and is so commodiously situated for the Indian trade, that from the first establishment of the colony it has been in a very flourishing condition, and maintained very early six hundred whites in that trade alone. The Indian nations on their borders are the upper and lower Creeks, the Chickesaws, and the Cherokees; who are some of the most numerous and powerful tribes in America. The trade of skins with this people is the largest we have, it takes in that of Georgia, the two Carolinas and Virginia. We deal with them somewhat in furs likewise, but they are of an inferior sort. All species of animals, that bear the fur, by a wise providence have it more thick, and of a softer and finer kind as you go to the northward; the greater the cold, the better they are clad.

CHAP. XXVII.

Nova Scotia, the time and reasons of its settlement. French there. Climate and soil. Annapolis, Halifax and Lunenburg.

THE last province we have settled, or rather began to settle, upon the continent of North America, is Nova Scotia.

This vaſt province, called by the French Acadie, has New England and the Atlantic ocean to the South and South-Weſt, and the river and gulph of St. Laurence to the North and North-Eaſt. It lies between the 44th and 50th degrees of North latitude, and though in a very favourable part of the temperate zone, has a winter of an almoſt inſupportable length and coldneſs, continuing at leaſt ſeven months in the year; to this immediately ſucceeds, without the intervention of any thing that may be called ſpring, a ſummer of an heat as violent as the cold, though of no long continuance; and they are wrapt in the gloom of a perpetual fog, even long after the ſummer ſeaſon has commenced. In moſt parts, the ſoil is thin and barren, the corn it produces of a ſhrivelled kind like rye, and the graſs intermixed with a cold ſpungy moſs. However it is not uniformly bad; there are tracts in Nova Scotia, which do not yield to the beſt land in New England.

Unpromiſing as this country is, yet neglecting all thoſe delightful tracts to the Southward, it was here that ſome of the firſt European ſettlements were made. The French ſeated themſelves here before they made any eſtabliſhment in Canada; but whatever unaccountable ignorance influenced their choice, the induſtry and vigour of that time deſerves our applauſe; for though they had infinitely more difficulties

difficulties to ftruggle with than we have at this day, and not the hundredth part of the fuccours from Europe, yet they fubfifted in a tolerable manner, and increafed largely; when the colony which in our days we have fixed there, if the fupport of the royal hand was withdrawn but for a moment, after all the immenfe fums which have been expended in its eftablifhment, would undoubtedly fink into nothing. It is with difficulty it fubfifts, even encouraged and fupported as it is. Yet the defign of eftablifhing a colony here, with whatever difficulties it might have been attended, was a very prudent meafure; for the French would undoubtedly have profited of our neglects, and have by fome means got this country into their hands, to the great annoyance of all our colonies, and to the great benefit both of their fifhery and their fugar iflands.

This country has frequently changed hands from one private proprietor to the other, and from the French to the Englifh nation, backward and forward; until the treaty of Utrecht eftablifhed our right in it finally; as the treaty of Aix la Chapelle confirmed it. But both were deficient in not afcertaining diftinctly what bounds this province ought to have. This was left to be adjufted by commiffaries. Whilft they were debating, the French built forts, and fecured fuch a part of the province as they were resolved to hold. I have not throughout this work chosen to enter into territorial disputes, because they convey very little private instruction, and do nothing at all towards the establishment of the public rights; yet it is difficult to avoid remarking, that the line which the French have drawn in Nova Scotia, is not only not drawn by any treaty, but that it is very apparently calculated to secure them these parts of the province which they value most, and at the same time to pay an apparent respect to the treaty of Utrecht by leaving us some part of Acadia.

The chief town we had formerly in this province, was called Annapolis Royal; but though the capital, it was a small place, wretchedly fortified, and yet worse built and inhabited. Here were stationed the remains of a regiment which continued there very little recruited since the reign of queen Anne; but though this place never flourished, it stood upon the very best harbour, as it is said, in North America; but it was not here, but on the South-East side of the peninsula, that the settlement, resolved and executed with so much spirit at the end of the last war, was established. This too stands upon a fine harbour, very commodiously situated, and rather better than Annapolis for the fishery. The town is called Halifax from the present earl, to whose wisdom and care we owe this settlement. In 1743,

1743, three thoufand families, at an immenfe charge to the government, were tranfported into this country at once, and (I think) three regiments ftationed there to protect them from the Indians, who have always fhewed themfelves our moft implacable enemies. The town is large, and for fo new a fettlement well built. It has a good intrenchment of timber, ftrengthened with forts of the fame materials, fo as to be in little danger at leaft from an Indian enemy.

Though this town of Halifax has, all things confidered, a tolerable appearance, the adjacent country is not improved in proportion; the ground is very hard to be cleared; when cleared does not produce a great deal, and labour is extravagantly dear. But this colony has fuffered more from the incurfions of the Indians than from any thing elfe. Their incurfions have been fo frequent, and attended with fuch cruelties, that the people can hardly extend themfelves beyond the cannon of the fort, nor attend their works of agriculture even there without the greateft danger. The confequence of this is, that they do not raife the fifth part of what is fufficient to maintain them. Moft of their provifion of every fort comes from New England, and they muft have ftarved if it were not for the fifhery, which it muft be owned is not contemptible, and for fome little naval ftores, and the pay of the garrison, the spending of which here is the principal use of the troops; against the Indian enemy they are of very little effect; though there are three regiments, and all the fighting men the Indians can raise in that propince are not five hundred. The soldiers, inactive by their confinement in their barracks, diseased for the most part with the scurvy, and debilitated by the use of spirituous liquors, are quite an undermatch for the activity, vigilance, patience, and address of the American. A company of wood rangers kept constantly to scour the country near our settlements, and a small body of Indians who might be brought at an easy rate from the friendly tribes who inhabit our other settlements, and encouraged by a reward for what scalps they should bring home, sent to infest the enemy amongst their own habitations, would have protected our colony, and long ago exterminated the Indians, or reduced them to an useful subjection, since unfortunately we have not the secret of gaining their affections. The easy plan I have mentioned would not have had half the expence attending it, that the maintainance of a numerous and almost useless garrison has had. A little experience will shew to the most ordinary understandings, what hardly any sagacity could have without it unveiled to the most penetrating statesman. It was a want of this experience that caused another mistake of almost

most as bad a nature. Until the beginning of this war a number of the ancient French colony, some say ten or twelve thousand souls, remained in the country, and were called and treated in a manner as a neutral people, though they ought to have been the king's subjects; but they yielded very little obedience to the crown of England, as in truth they had from us very little protection, and they were even accused of encouraging the Indian incursions, and supplying them with arms and ammunition to annoy our people. Had we erected in their country a little fort, and in it kept a small garrison, to be maintained by that people themselves, appointed magistrates, and made them know the benefit and excellency of the British laws, and at the same time impressed them with a dread of the British power, we might have saved many useful people to this colony, and prevented the necessity (if it was a necessity) of using measures, which, if they are not impolitic, are certainly such as an humane and generous mind is never constrained to but with regret.

Besides Annapolis and Halifax, we have another settlement a little to the South-West of the latter, called Lunenburg. This is a branch of Germans from Halifax, who being discontented at the infertility of the soil there, desired to go where there was better land to be had, undertaking their own defence; accordingly

cordingly they settled where they desired, to the number of seven or eight hundred, and succeed tolerably well. Upon a tumult which arose amongst them, the governor sent a party of soldiers to protect them from their own discords, and from the enemy. This province is yet but in its beginning, and therefore, except in prospect, can afford us no great subject matter of speculation.

CHAP. XXVIII.

The island of Newfoundland. The fishery there. The Bermudas. Their settlement and trade. The Bahamas.

TO the East of this province lies the great isle of Newfoundland, above three hundred miles long, and two hundred broad, extending quite up to New Britain, and forming the Eastern boundary of the gulf of St. Laurence. This island, after various disputes about the property, was entirely ceded to England by the treaty of Utrecht. From the soil of this island we were far from reaping any sudden or great advantage; for the cold is long continued and intense; and the summer heat, though violent, warms it not enough to produce any thing valuable; for the soil, at least in those parts of the island with which we are acquainted, (for we are far from knowing

ing the whole) is rocky and barren. However, it hath many large and safe harbours; and several good rivers water it. This island, whenever the continent shall come to fail of timber convenient to navigation, (which perhaps is no very remote prospect) will afford a copious supply for masts, yards, and all sorts of lumber for the West-India trade. But what at present it is chiefly valuable for, is the great fishery of cod, which is carried on upon those shoals which are called the banks of Newfoundland. In that the French and Spaniards, especially the former, have a large share. Our share of this fishery is computed to increase the national stock by three hundred thousand a year, in gold and silver, remitted us for the cod we sell in the North, in Spain, Portugal, Italy and the Levant. The plenty of cod, both on the great bank and the lesser ones which lie to the East and South East of this island, is inconceivable; and not only cod, but several other species of fish are there in abundance; all these species are nearly in an equal plenty all along the shores of New England, Nova Scotia, and the isle of Cape Breton; and consequently excellent fisheries are carried on upon all their coasts. Where our American colonies are so ill peopled, or so barren as not to produce any thing from their soil, their coasts make us ample amends; and pour in upon us a wealth of
another

another kind, and no way inferior to the former, from their fisheries.

We have in North America, besides this, two clusters of islands; the Bermudas or Summer islands, at a vast distance from the continent in lat. 31. and the Bahama islands. The former were very early settled, and were much celebrated in the time of the civil wars, when several of the cavalier party being obliged to retire into America, some of them, in particular Mr. Waller, the poet, spent some time in this island. Waller was extremely enamoured with the serenity of the air, and the beauty and richness of the vegetable productions of these islands; he celebrated them in a poem, which is fine but unequal, which he wrote upon this subject.

The Bermudas are but small; not containing in all upwards of twenty thousand acres. They are very difficult of access, being, as Waller expresses it, walled with rocks. What has been said of the clearness and serenity of the air, and of the healthiness of the climate, was not exaggerated; but the soil could never boast of an extraordinary fertility. Their best production was cedar, which was superior to any thing of the kind in America. It is still so, though diminished considerably in quantity, which has, as it is imagined, changed the air much for the worse; for now it is much

much more inconstant than formerly; and several tender vegetables, which flourished here at the first settlement, being deprived of their shelter, and exposed to the bleak Northerly winds, are seen no more.

The chief, and indeed only business of these islanders, is the building and navigating light sloops, and brigantines, built with their cedar, which they employ chiefly in the trade between North America and the West-Indies. These vessels are as remarkable for their swiftness, as the wood of which they are built is for its hard and durable quality. They export nothing from themselves but some white stone to the West-Indies, and some of their garden productions. To England they send nothing. Formerly they made a good deal of money of a sort of hats for womens wear of the leaves of their palmetto's, which whilst the fashion lasted were elegant; but the trade and the fashion are gone together.

Their whites are computed to be about five thousand, the blacks which they breed are the best in America, and as useful as the whites in their navigation. The people of the Bermudas are poor, but healthy, contented, and remarkably chearful. It is extremely surprising that they do not set themselves heartily to the cultivation of vines in this island, to which their rocky soil seems admirably adapted; and their situation and the manner of trade

they

they are already engaged in, would facilitate the diftribution of their wine to every part of North America and the Weft-Indies.

The Bahamas are fituated to the South of Carolina, from lat. 22 to 27, and they extend along the coaft of Florida quite down to the Ifle of Cuba; and are faid to be five hundred in number; fome of them only mere rocks; but a great many others large, fertile, and in nothing differing from the foil of Carolina. All are however abfolutely uninhabited, except Providence, which is neither the largeft nor the moft fertile.

This ifland was formerly a receptacle for the pirates, who for a long time infefted the American navigation. This obliged the government to erect a fort there, to ftation an independent company in the ifland, and to fend thither a governor. This ifland has at prefent not much trade, fome oranges it fends to North America excepted. However, in time of war it makes confiderably by the prizes condemned here, and in time of peace by the wrecks, which are frequent in this labyrinth of innumerable rocks and fhelves.

This is all the benefit we derive from fo many large and fertile iflands, fituated in fuch a climate as will produce any thing, and which as it is never reached by any frofts, would yield in all probability even fugars, of as good a fort, and in as great abundance, as any iflands

in

in the West-Indies. Nothing more fully shews the present want of that spirit of adventure and enterprize, which was so common in the two last centuries, and which is of such infinite honour and advantage to any time or nation, than that these islands so situated can lie unoccupied, whilst we complain of the want of land proper for sugar, and whilst an hundred pounds an acre is sometimes paid for such in the Caribbees. This point, to any who will be at the pains of studying the situation of these islands, and the consequences which may result from the improvement or neglect of them, will appear of no small importance: and perhaps an enquiry into the causes of the strange degree of backwardness in which they are at present, may be a very prudent and perhaps a necessary measure.

CHAP. XXIX.

Hudson's Bay. Attempts for the discovery of a North-West passage. The Hudson's bay company. Thoughts upon its trade. Climate and soil of the countries there. Conclusion.

THE countries about Hudson's and Baffin's Bay make the last object of our speculation in America. The knowledge of these seas was owing to a project for the discovery of a North-West passage to China.

So early as the year 1576 this noble defign was conceived; fince then it has been frequently dropped; it has often been revived; it is not yet compleated; but was never defpaired of by thofe whofe knowledge and fpirit make them competent judges and lovers of fuch undertakings. Frobifher only difcovered the main of New Britain, or Terra de Labrador, and thofe ftraits to which he has given his name. In 1585 John David failed from Dartmouth, and viewed that and the more Northerly coafts; but he feems never to have entered the bay.

Hudfon made three voyages on the fame adventure, the firft in 1607, the fecond in 1608, and his third and laft in 1610. This bold and judicious navigator entered the ftraits that led into this new Mediterranean, coafted a great part of it, and penetrated to eighty degrees twenty-three minutes into the heart of the frozen zone. His ardor for the difcovery, not abated by the difficulties he ftruggled with in this empire of winter, and world of froft and fnow, he ftaid here until the enfuing fpring, and prepared in the beginning of 1611 to purfue his difcoveries; but his crew, who fuffered equal hardfhips, without the fame fpirit to fupport them, mutinied, feized upon him and feven of thofe who were moft faithful to him, and committed them to the fury of the feas in an
open

open boat. Hudson and his companions were either swallowed up by the waves, or gaining the inhospitable coast which they water, were destroyed by the savages; but his fate so calamitous cannot so much discourage a generous mind from such undertakings, as the immortality of his name, which he has secured by having given it to so great a sea, will be a spur to others to expect an equal honour, and perhaps with better success.

From the first voyage of Frobisher an hundred and ten years ago, to that of captain Ellis, notwithstanding so many disappointments, the rational hopes of this grand discovery have grown greater by every attempt, and seem to spring even out of our very failures. The greater swell of the tides in the inner part of the bay than near the straits, an appearance so unknown in any other inland seas, and the increase of this swell with Westerly winds, seems without any other arguments to evince the certain existence of such a passage as we have so long sought without success.

But though we have hitherto failed in the original purpose for which we navigated this bay, yet such great designs even in their failures bestow a sufficient reward for whatever has been expended upon them. In 1670 the charter was granted to a company for the exclusive trade to this bay, and they have

have acted under it ever since with great benefit to the private men who compose the company, though comparatively with little advantage to Great Britain. It is true that their trade in beavers and other species of furs is not inconsiderable, and it is a trade in itself of the best kind; its object enters largely into our manufactures, and carries nothing but our manufactures from us to procure it; and thus it has the qualities of the most advantageous kinds of traffic. The company has besides pretty large returns in beaver and deer skins. It is said that the dividends of this company are prodigious; far exceeding what is gained in any of the other great trading bodies; yet their capital is small, they seem little inclined to enlarge their bottom, and appear strongly possessed with that spirit of jealousy that prevails in some degree in all knots and societies of men endued with peculiar privileges. The officers of the company have behaved to those who wintered within their jurisdiction in search of the North-West passage (one of the purposes for which the company itself was originally instituted) in such a manner as to give us the truest idea of this spirit. If I had been singular in this opinion, I should have expressed my sentiments with much greater diffidence; but this abuse has been often and loudly complained of. It would appear astonishing that this trade has not hitherto been

laid

laid open, if in the perplexing multiplicity of affairs that engages our miniſtry, ſomething muſt not neceſſarily paſs unredreſſed.

The vaſt countries which ſurround this Bay all abound with animals, whoſe fur is excellent, and ſome of kinds which are not yet brought into commerce; and the company is very far from any attempt to ſtretch this trade to its full extent. If the trade were laid open, it ſeems of neceſſity that three capital advantages would enſue: firſt, that the trade going into a number of rival hands, with a more moderate profit to individuals, it would conſume a much greater quantity of our manufactures, employ more of our ſhipping and ſeamen, and of courſe bring home more furs, and by lowering the price of that commodity at home, increaſe the demand of thoſe manufactures into which they enter at the foreign markets; it might bring home other ſpecies of furs than thoſe we deal in at preſent, and thus open new channels of trade, which in commerce is a matter of great conſideration. Secondly, this more general intercourſe would make the country better known; it would habituate great numbers of our people to it; it would diſcover the moſt tolerable parts for a ſettlement; and thus, inſtead of a miſerable fort or two, time might ſhew an Engliſh colony at Hudſon's Bay, which would open the fur trade yet more fully, and increaſe the vent of our manufactures yet further. Thirdly, this more general trade on the Bay would naturally, without any new expence or trouble whatsoever, in a very short space of time discover to us the so much desired North-West passage, or shew us clearly and definitively that we ought to expect no such thing. These advantages, and even yet more considerable ones, would be derived from laying open this trade under such proper regulations, which the nature of the object would point out of itself.

No colony has been hitherto attempted at Hudson's Bay. The company has two inconsiderable forts there. The country is every where barren; to the Northward of the bay even the hardy pine tree is seen no longer, and the cold womb of the earth is incapable of any better production than some miserable shrubs. The winter reigns with an inconceiveable rigour for near nine months of the year; the other three are violently hot, except when the North-West wind renews the memory of the winter. Every kind of European seed, which we have committed to the earth in this inhospitable climate, has hitherto perished; but in all probability we have not tried the seed of corn from the Northern parts of Sweden and Norway; in such cases the place from whence the seed comes is of great moment. All this severity and long continuance of winter, and the barrenness of the earth, which arises from thence, is experienced,

rienced, in the latitude of 51; in the temperate latitude of Cambridge. However, it is far from increafing uniformly as you go Northwards. Captain James wintered in Charlton ifland, in latitude 51; he judged that the climate here was to be deemed utterly uninhabitable on account of the furprifing hardfhips which he fuffered; yet the company has a fort feveral degrees more to the Northward, where their fervants make a fhift to fubfift tolerably. It is called Fort Nelfon, and is in the latitude 54.

All the animals of thefe countries are cloathed with a clofe, foft, warm fur. In fummer there is here, as in other places, a variety in the colours of the feveral animals; when that is over they all affume the livery of winter, and every fort of beafts, and moft of their fowls, are of the colour of the fnow, every thing animate and inanimate is white. This is a furprifing phenomenon. But what is yet more furprifing, and what is indeed one of thefe ftriking things that draw the moft inattentive to an admiration of the wifdom and goodnefs of Providence, is, that the dogs and cats from England, that have been carried into Hudfon's Bay, on the approach of winter have intirely changed their appearance, and acquired a much longer, fofter, and thicker coat of hair than they had originally. As for the men of the country, Providence there, as every where elfe, has given them no provision but their own art and ingenuity, and they shew a great deal in their manner of kindling a fire, in cloathing themselves, and in preserving their eyes from the ill effects of that glaring white that every where surrounds them for the greatest part of the year; in other respects they are very savage. In their shapes and faces, they do not resemble the Americans who live to the Southward; they are much more like the Laplanders and Samoeids of Europe, from whom they are probably descended. The other Americans seem to be of a Tartar original.

I have now finished upon my plan the survey of the English colonies in America. I flatter myself that so full an idea has not been given of them before in so narrow a compass. By this the reader will himself be enabled to judge, for it is not my design to preoccupy his judgment in these particulars, how our colonies have grown, what their vegetative principle has been, in what vigour it subsists, or what signs of corruption appear in any of them; how far we have pursued the advantages which our situation, and the nature of the country have given us; or where we have pursued them, whether we have gone to the ultimate point. He will see how far the colonies have served the trade of the mother country, and how much the mother country has done or neglected to do towards their happiness and prosperity. Certainly our colonies deserve,
and

and would fully reward an attention of a very different kind from any that has ever yet been given to them. Even as they are circumstanced, I do not in the least hesitate to say that we derive more advantage, and of a better kind, from our colonies, than the Spaniards and Portuguese have from theirs, abounding as they are with gold and silver and precious stones; although in ours there is no appearance at all of such dazzling and delusive wealth. But then I conceive it might be made very clear, that had they yielded us these splendid medals in lieu of what they now produce, the effect would be far less to our advantage. Our present intercourse with them is an emulation in industry; they have nothing that does not arise from theirs, and what we receive enters into our manufactures, excites our industry, and increases our commerce; whereas gold is the measure or account, but not the means of trade. And it is found in nations as it is in the fortunes of private men, that what does not arise from labour, but is acquired by other means, is never lasting. Such acquisitions extinguish industry, which is alone the parent of any solid riches.

The barbarism of our ancestors could not comprehend how a nation could grow more populous by sending out a part of its people. We have lived to see this paradox made out by experience, but we have not sufficiently profited of this experience; since we begin, some of us at least, to think that there is a danger of dispeopling ourselves by encouraging new colonies, or increasing the old. If our colonies find, as hitherto they have constantly done, employment for a great number of hands, there is no danger but that hands will be found for the employment. That a rich, trading and manufacturing nation should be long in want of people, is a most absurd supposition; for besides that the people within themselves multiply the most where the means of subsistence are most certain, it is as natural for people to flock into a busy and wealthy country, that by any accident may be thin of people, as it is for the dense air to rush into those parts where it is rarified. He must be a great stranger to this country, who does not observe in it a vast number of people, whose removal from hence, if they could be of any use elsewhere, would prove of very little detriment to the public.

I have already observed, that the trade of our colonies deserves a more particular attention than any other, not only on account of the advantages I have just mentioned, but because our attention is sure of being sufficiently rewarded. The object is in our own power; it is of a good kind; and of such extent and variety, as to employ nobly the most inven-

tive

tive genius in thofe matters. Foreign politics have fomething more fplendid and entertaining than domeftic prudence; but this latter is ever attended, though with lefs glaring, yet with infinitely more folid, fecure, and lafting advantages. The great point of our regard in America, ought therefore to be the effectual peopling, employment, and ftrength of our poffeffions there; in a fubordinate degree the management of our interefts with regard to the French and Spaniards. The latter we have reafon to refpect, to indulge, and even perhaps to endure; and more, it is probable, may be had from them in that way than by the violent methods which fome have fo warmly recommended, and ftill urge, tho' we have had fome experience to convince us of their infufficiency. But the nature of the French, their fituation, their defigns, every thing has fhewn that we ought to ufe every method to reprefs them, to prevent them from extending their territories, their trade, or their influence, and above all to connive at not the leaft encroachment; but this in fuch a manner as not to ftrain our own ftrength, or turn our eyes from ferving ourfelves by attempts to diftrefs them. But as we are now in the midft of a war, until that is decided, it will be impoffible to fay any thing fatisfactory on our connections with French America, until we see what the next treaty of peace will do in the diftribution of the territory of the two nations there.

CHAP. XXX.

The royal, proprietary, and charter governments. Laws of the colonies. Paper currency. Abufes in it. Another fort of money propofed.

THE fettlement of our colonies was never purfued upon any regular plan; but they were formed, grew, and flourifhed, as accidents, the nature of the climate, or the difpofitions of private men happened to operate. We ought not therefore to be furprifed to find in the feveral conftitutions and governments of our colonies, fo little of any thing like uniformity. It has been faid that there is fcarce any form of government known, that does not prevail in fome of our plantations; the variety is certainly great and vicious; but the latitude of the obfervation muft be fomewhat reftrained; for fome forms they are certainly ftrangers to. To pafs over feveral, nothing like a pure hereditary ariftocracy has ever appeared in any of them.

The firft colony which we fettled, was that of Virginia. It was governed for fome time by a prefident and a council, appointed by the crown;

crown; but when the people were increased to a considerable body, it was not thought reasonable to leave them longer under a mode of government so averse from that which they had enjoyed at home. They were therefore empowered to elect representatives for the several counties into which this province is divided, with privileges resembling those of the representatives of the commons in England. The persons so elected form what is called the lower house of assembly. This was added to the council which still subsisted, and the members of which were, and to this day are nominated by the crown, as at the first, and they are not only nominated by the crown but hold their seats during the king's pleasure, as signified by his governor. They are stiled honourable, and are chosen from the persons of the best fortunes and most considerable influence in the country. They form another branch of the legislature, and are sometimes called the upper house of assembly. They answer in some measure to the house of peers in our constitution. As the lower house of assembly is the guardian of the people's privileges, the council is appointed chiefly to preserve the prerogative of the crown, and to secure the dependence of the colony; it is the more effectually to answer these ends, that the members of the council only are appointed during pleasure.

When

When any bill has paſſed the two houſes, it comes before the governor, who repreſents the king, and gives his aſſent or negative, as he thinks proper. It now acquires the force of a law, but it muſt be afterwards tranſmitted to the king and council in England, where it may ſtill receive a negative that takes away all its effect. The upper houſe of aſſembly not only forms a part of the legiſlature of the colony, but it acts as a privy council to the governor, without whoſe concurrence, he can do nothing of moment; it ſometimes acts as a court of chancery. This is the common form of government, and the beſt too that is in uſe in the plantations. This is the manner of government in all the iſlands of the Weſt-Indies; in Nova Scotia; in one province of New England, and with ſome reſtriction, in another; in New York, New Jerſey, Virginia, the two Carolinas, and Georgia. This form is commonly called a royal government.

The ſecond form in uſe in our ſettlements in America is called a proprietary government. At our firſt planting that part of the world, it was not difficult for a perſon who had intereſt at court, to obtain large tracts of land, not inferior in extent to many kingdoms; and to be inveſted with a power very little leſs than regal over them; to govern by what laws, and to form what ſort of conſtitution he pleaſed. A dependence upon the crown of England

England was shewn only by the payment of an Indian arrow, a few skins, or some other trifling acknowledgment of the same nature. We had formerly many more governments of that sort, than we have at present; in the West-Indies, the island of Barbadoes was granted to the earl of Carlisle; and we have seen a like grant made of the island of St. Lucia to the duke of Montague in this age, which after an infinite charge to that benevolent nobleman came to nothing, by a sort of tacit allowance of the French claim to it. This was in 1722, when our connection with France hindered us from exerting our rights with the necessary vigour. Carolina was formerly a government of this kind, but it was lodged in eight proprietaries. How they parted with their rights we have seen already. New Jersey was likewise a proprietary government; but this too failed like the others. The only governments in this form which remain at present, but considerably abridged of their privileges, are Pensilvania and Maryland. In the latter the constitution exactly resembles that of the royal governments; a governor, council, and assembly of the representatives of the people; but the governor is appointed by the proprietary, and approved by the crown. The customs are reserved to the crown likewise; and the officers belonging to them are independent of the government of the

the province. In Penfylvania the proprietary is under the fame reftrictions that limit the proprietary of Maryland, on the fide of the crown; on the fide of the people, he is yet more reftrained; for their legiflature has but two parts, the affembly of the people and the governor; fo that the governor wanting the great influence which the council gives in other places, whenever his fentiments differ from thofe of the affembly, he is engaged in a very unequal conteft.

The third form is called a charter government; this originally prevailed in all the provinces of New England; and ftill remains in two of them, Connecticut and Rhode Ifland. By the charters to thefe colonies, the exorbitant power which was given in the proprietary governments to fingle men, was here vefted, and I apprehend much more dangeroufly, in the whole body of the people. It is to all purpofes a mere democracy. They elect every one of their own officers, from the higheft to the loweft; they difplace them at pleafure; and the laws which they enact, are valid without the royal approbation. This ftate of unbounded freedom, I believe, contributed in fome degree to make thofe fettlements flourifh; but it certainly contributed as much to render their value to their mother country far more precarious, than a better digefted plan would have done that might have taken in the

the interests both of Great Britain and of the new settlement. The truth is, nothing of an enlarged and legislative spirit appears in the planning of our colonies; the charter governments were evidently copied from some of our corporations at home, which if they are good institutions themselves, yet are by no means fit to be imitated by a new people going into a remote country, far from the eye and hand of the supreme power. What may be an useful institution for an inferior member of some great body, and closely united to it, may be not at all proper for a new settlement, which is to form a sort of dependent commonwealth in a remote part of the world. Here the ends to be answered, are to make the new establishment as useful as possible to the trade of the mother country; to secure its dependence; to provide for the ease, safety, and happiness of the settlers; to protect them from their enemies, and to make an easy and effectual provision to preserve them from the tyranny and avarice of their governors, or the ill consequences of their own licentiousness; that they should not, by growing into an unbounded liberty, forget that they were subjects, or lying under a base servitude have no reason to think themselves British subjects. This is all that colonies, according to the present and best ideas of them, can or ought to be. The charter governments

ments had nothing of this in view, and consequently provided for it but very indifferently.

The province of Massachusets Bay, which is partly a government of this popular kind, but tempered with something more of the royal authority, seems to be on still a worse footing, through the one error of having no established provision for the governor; this one mischief is productive of a thousand others, because the governor in a manner is obliged to keep intrigues and devices on foot, to reconcile the various parts which he must act, and is necessitated to govern by faction and cabal. Hence it is that the charges of this one government are greater than those not only of the other provinces of New England taken together, but of those of Pensylvania and New York added to them; they are deeply in debt, they are every day plunging deeper, their taxes increase, and their trade declines.

It has been an old complaint, that it is not easy to bring American governors to justice for mismanagements in their province, or to make them refund to the injured people the wealth raised by their extortions. Against such governors at present there are three kinds of remedy; the privy council, the king's bench, and the parliament. The council on just cause of complaint may remove the governor; the power of the council seems to extend no further.

ther. The king's bench may punish the governors for their offences committed in America, as if done in England. The power of parliament is unlimited in the ways of enquiry into the crime, or of punishing it. The first of these remedies can never be sufficient to terrify a governor grown rich by iniquity, and willing to retire quietly, though dishonourably, to enjoy the fruits of it. The king's bench, or any other merely law court, seems equally insufficient for this purpose, because offences in government, though very grievous, can hardly ever be so accurately defined as to be a proper object of any court of justice, bound up by forms and the rigid letter of the law. The parliament is equal to every thing; but whether party, and other bars to a quick and effectual proceeding may not here leave the provinces as much unredressed as in the other courts, I shall not take upon me to determine.

The law in all our provinces, besides those acts which from time to time they have made for themselves, is the common law of England, the old statute law, and a great part of the new, which in looking over their laws I find many of our settlements have adopted, with very little choice or discretion. And indeed the laws of England, if in the long period of their duration they have had many improvements, so they have grown more tedious, perplexed, and intricate, by the heaping

ing up many abuses in one age, and the attempts to remove them in another. These infant settlements surely demanded a more simple, clear, and determinate legislation, though it were of somewhat an homelier kind; laws suited to the time, to their country, and the nature of their new way of life. Many things still subsist in the law of England, which are built upon causes and reasons that have long ago ceased; many things are in those laws suitable to England only. But the whole weight of this ill-agreeing mass, which neither we nor our fathers were well able to bear, is laid upon the shoulders of these colonies, by which a spirit of contention is raised, and arms offensive and defensive are supplied to keep up and exercise this spirit, by the intricacy and unsuitableness of the laws to their object. And thus in many of our settlements the lawyers have gathered to themselves the greatest part of the wealth of the country; men of less use in such establishments than in more settled countries, where the number of people naturally sets many apart from the occupations of husbandry, arts, or commerce. Certainly our American brethren might well have carried with them the privileges which make the glory and happiness of Englishmen, without taking them encumbered with all that load of matter, perhaps so useless at home, without doubt so extremely prejudicial in the colonies. Laws

Laws themselves are hardly more the cement of societies than money; and societies flourish or decay according to the condition of either of these. It may be easily judged, that as the balance of trade with Great Britain is very much against the colonies, that therefore whatever gold or silver they may receive from the other branches of their commerce, makes but a short stay in America. This consideration at first view would lead one to conclude, that in a little time money for their ordinary circulation would be wanting; and this is apparently confirmed by experience. Very little money is seen amongst them, notwithstanding the vast increase of their trade. This deficiency is supplied, or more properly speaking, it is caused by the use of money of credit, which they commonly call paper currency. This money is not created for the conveniency of traffic, but by the exigencies of the government, and often by the frauds and artifices of private men for their particular profit. Before this invention money was indeed scarce enough in America, but they raised its value, and it served their purpose tolerably. I shall forbear entering into the causes that increased the charges of government so greatly in all our American provinces. But the execution of projects too vast for their strength, made large sums necessary. The feeble state of a colony which had hardly taken root in the country, could not bear them; and to raise sudden and heavy taxes, would destroy the province without answering their purpose. Credit then came in aid of money, and the government issued bills to the amount of what they wanted, to pass current in all payments; and they commonly laid a tax, or found some persons willing to engage their lands as security for the gradual sinking this debt, and calling in these bills. But before the time arrived at which these taxes were to answer their end, new exigencies made new emissions of paper currency necessary; and thus things went from debt to debt, until it became very visible that no taxes which could be imposed could discharge them; and that the land securities given were often fraudulent, and almost always insufficient. Then the paper currency became no longer to be weighed against the credit of the government, which depended upon its visible revenue. It was compared to the trade, to which it was found so disproportionate, that the bills fell ten, twenty, fifty, and eighty per cent in some places. It was to no purpose that the government used every method to keep up their credit, and even to compel the receiving these bills at the value for which they were emitted, and to give no preference over them to gold and silver; they were more and more depreciated every day; whilst the government every day emitted more paper, and grew

grew less sollicitous about their old bills, being entirely exhausted to find means of giving credit to the new.

It is easy to perceive how much the intercourse of business must suffer by this uncertainty in the value of money, when a man receives that in payment this day for ten shillings, which to-morrow he will not find received from him for five, or perhaps for three. Real money can hardly ever multiply too much in any country, because it will always as it increases be the certain sign of the increase of trade, of which it is the measure, and consequently of the soundness and vigour of the whole body. But this paper money may, and does increase, without any increase of trade, nay often when it greatly declines, for it is not the measure of the trade of the nation, but of the necessity of its government; and it is absurd, and must be ruinous, that the same cause which naturally exhausts the wealth of a nation, should likewise be the only productive cause of money.

The currency of our plantations must not be set upon a level with the funds in England. For besides that the currency carries no interest to make some amends for the badness of the security; the security itself is so rotten, that no art can give it any lasting credit; as there are parts of New England wherein, if the whole stock and the people along with it were

were sold, they would not bring money enough to take in all the bills which have been emitted.

I hope it is not too late to contrive some remedy for this evil, as those at the head of affairs here are undoubtedly very sollicitous about so material a grievance. I should imagine that one current coin for the whole continent might be struck here, or there, with such an alloy as might at once leave it of some real value, and yet so debased as to prevent its currency elsewhere, and so to keep it within themselves. This expedient has been practised, and with success, in several parts of Europe; but particularly in Holland, a country which undoubtedly is perfectly acquainted with its commercial interest.

F I N I S.

www.ingramcontent.com/pod-product-compliance
Lightning Source LLC
Chambersburg PA
CBHW022019240426
43667CB00042B/945